GERMAN PAINTING

Library of Congress Catalog Card Number 59-13044

PRINTED IN FRANCE

MARCEL BRION

GERMAN PAINTING

Translated by
W. J. STRACHAN

UNIVERSE BOOKS, INC. · NEW YORK
ÉDITIONS PIERRE TISNÉ · PARIS

It is impossible to cover the history of painting in the Germanic countries for a period of roughly seven centuries in a single volume without certain sacrifices.

It means confining oneself to easel-pictures; and the study of mural or miniature painting, together with that of engraving, interdependent though painting and engraving were, particularly in the sixteenth century, must of necessity be omitted.

Nor will space allow a consideration of certain problems of development; only main trends can be dealt with and a number of interesting artists will have to be left out.

The problem was still further complicated by the fact that in an account which embraced countries such as Czechoslovakia, Switzerland and Austria, proud of their independence and autonomy, it was essential to avoid the impression that these countries had, at any time, depended on Germany for the vitality, richness and beauty of their art. In all matters of art any claim to nationalism is absurd and dishonest, for a painter or even a "school" is closely bound up with aesthetic forms cultivated in other countries in every period and every circumstance.

The introducing of Czechoslovakian, Austrian and Swiss painters in a work entitled *German Painting* in no way indicates a denial or misunderstanding of the genuinely original and personal elements in Czechoslovakian, Austrian and Swiss painting, but merely underlines the mutual contributions and exchanges which have taken place through the centuries. There is no such thing as German art — any more than there is French or Italian art — narrowly contained within political or geographical boundaries, and in Germany, as everywhere else, art has always been the richer for being open to foreign influences. This does not mean that it should adopt a systematic cosmopolitanism or deny its national spirit or its own character in favor of an eclecticism, which, in this case, would be artificial and superficial. As the book proceeds, it will be possible to trace the continual links which connect Germanic artists with the other European centers. The French in the fifteenth and at the close of the nineteenth century, the Italians in their Renaissance and Baroque periods, the Flemish in the sixteenth and seventeenth centuries, played a dominating part in the development of German art and the direction it took at certain turning points in its history; of this there can be no doubt.

Far from claiming to fix the boundaries of a closed aesthetic unity, the present work aims at exploring the paths which German art, firmly rooted in its own soil, has followed in its search for life-bringing sustenance on every side which it has transformed into something truly personal, original and alive. Furthermore it should not be difficult to recognize from one century to the next the persistence of certain constants, characteristic of German art and to which it remains faithful, consciously or unconsciously, even under pressure from temptation in other countries.

In view of the lack of space to discuss problems of attribution — always thorny and permanently arguable — the present author has preferred not to involve the reader in these disputes, and among the choices possible he has, on each occasion, chosen the conclusion reached by the most eminent specialists whose opinions are considered authoritative.

THE moment when *easel*, as opposed to mural painting — the latter closely identified with architecture and sculpture — arose in Germany coincides with the movement of medieval art towards an aesthetic conception less narrowly dependent on the religious program which dominated the Middle Ages. Functional considerations were, even more than aesthetic, responsible, it is true, for the shifting of painting from the wall at a time when walls were providing gaps for wide and lofty windows. It will however be noted that although painting deserted walls for altarpieces, it did not break away from its architectural and painted context, since the particular nature of the easel-painting, especially in its earlier stages, involves the close association of painted panels, gilded and polychromatic carving and elaborate frames with architectural motifs, likewise gilded and painted.

This art may be called "mannerist" in a great number of its manifestations, imbued as it is with the spirit of the later Middle Ages when Gothic art generally was exhausting itself in a complication of more violent and exteriorized forms. An art emanating from princely courts or those of the new merchant class was eager and ready to shake off the yoke of strict spirituality. A new sense of form appeared in profane art and had immediate repercussions on religious art.

Thus it was that the typical mannerist idiom of the last phase of Gothic art while throwing open its doors to exterior, sensual and almost pagan beauty still remained imbued with an intense and authentic spirituality. Court art and the art patronized by merchant class and church were thus blended in varying proportions and resulted in extremely original and attractive combinations in the different "Provinces" where Germanic art held sway in the fourteenth and fifteenth century. It is impossible to describe the way the various "schools", each informed with the spirit and idiom of its own region and evolving its own aesthetics, are constituted in this easel-painting, unless we bear in mind that the studios of a town or province never worked in isolation. Indeed, rarely in the course of history have more journeys been made and had more far-reaching effects than during the last phase of the Middle Ages and the beginning of the Renaissance.

WESTPHALIA

It was at Soest in Westphalia, a rich and powerful town with very strong artistic traditions, that painting on wood panels first replaced the vast ensembles of frescoes and ambitious compositions of the great stained glass window masters. It was more mobile painting at a time when the space accorded stained glass left less and less room for mural decorations and was therefore well adapted to the setting up on altars of folding altarpieces and polyptychs with wings which, in their turn, developed into veritable edifices inside fifteenth and sixteenth century churches.

The altarpiece provided the Westphalian school with a new outlet for its art, and we first notice the appearance of painted oak panels at the beginning of the thirteenth century. They are still crude works and not to be compared with the excellence of Romanesque frescoes with their rare and impressive beauty. It was however from these creative pieces of craftsmanship that the first noteworthy painting of Soest, the Wiesenkirche predella of 1376, emerged; but it is not until thirty more years have passed that we become aware that, under the influence of a master of outstanding genius, Master Konrad, of whose origins and education nothing is known, a characteristically Westphalian style has been established. Of this artist's work the only date of which we can be certain is the year 1404, inscribed along with his signature on the back of the altarpiece of the Stadtkirche of Niederwildungen in Waldeck.

The Museum of Munster in Westphalia is rich in the works of Konrad von Soest and his school; there in his fertile eclecticism we can see the development of a composite aesthetic system from which the Master's pictorial style gradually evolves. His first undisputed work, the triumphal cross of the church of St. Patrocles in Soest, is a painted cross of a type very common in Italy, and it is not beyond the bounds of possibility that Konrad was inspired by Siennese or Tuscan models. It is nevertheless a long way from the realism of a Giotto. Conrad's personal genius is movingly and unmistakably revealed however in the majesty and wonderful unreality of a figure almost reduced to a symbol. Thus a certain intellectualism marks the beginnings of Westphalian painting at a period when, simultaneously, Bohemia and Northern Germany were striving towards the expression of material truth and physical illusion, as we see it, for example, in Master Theodoric and Master Bertram.

Westphalian style, on the contrary, as inaugurated by Konrad von Soest, is a combination of the desire to represent things as they are with the aim of disembodying to a certain extent the heroes of holy writ. If we know nothing of the details of Konrad's life, we have the evidence of his paintings that he worked in a Flemish-Burgundian milieu, as is shown by the costumes, accessories and architecture. Connections have been inferred, justifiably it seems to me, between the Westphalian painter and Melchior Broederlam, the best proof of which lies in the complicated and fantastic architecture of the elaborately worked canopied thrones. There remains nevertheless a great contrast in the central panel of the altarpiece as well as in the wings between the almost overwhelming importance lent to costumes that are extravagant in splendor and originality and the modest realism of the familiar detail. In Konrad von Soest lay hidden a cosmopolitan who in his adolescence had marvelled at the luxury and refinements of the Court of Burgundy. In the tender regard he shows for objects of everyday life that others would consider commonplace he is also a German. His brush caresses the modest drugget with a delicate grey and, with a warm brown, woods that are light in color or patinated by hands that have scoured them for so many long years.

Konrad von Soest gives equal proof of his striking knowledge of composition from which any sign of clumsiness or archaism has now been banished. The *Crucifixion* of Niederwildungen is a pyramidal construction on intersecting diagonals which reveal a very sure comprehension of space and spatial expression; the congestion which arises from crowding too many people in a confined area, forced the artist to resort to devices of superposition and spacing, and these correspond to extremely personal solutions, invented by the artist to get over the spatial problems involved. Remembering the outstanding characteristics of this knowledge and skill peculiar to Konrad, over and above the evidence of the signed Niederwildungen altarpiece, critics have attempted to pick out this Master's works from other products of the Soest school which up to the sixteenth century remained scrupulously faithful to its own teachings. In them we discern that mixture of homely realism and fantastic elegance, already observed in the Niederwildungen altarpiece but with less control of the composition, less originality, until finally the very real and attractive charm of Master Konrad becomes almost commonplace in the work of his followers.

Konrad von Soest's influence and that of the Westphalian School extended also to Lower Saxony and Hanover. The *Crucifixion* in the church of St. Lambert in Hildesheim (circa 1420) is clearly a prolongation of this influence, and we observe in it all the traits characteristic of Konrad, including his reminiscences of Flanders and Burgundy. The Göttingen *Crucifixion*, attributed to Heinrich von Duderstadt (circa 1424, Welfenmuseum, Hanover) also has pretty close affinities with it; likewise the famous *Güldene Tafel* (the "Golden Panel") in the same museum, which dates back to about 1410. The influence of the miniature on this noble polyptych, with its familiar, picturesque and moving details, is probably more recognizable than on other examples — the *Nativity* panel shows this particularly — and note, too, the frank and sober emotion in the panel representing the *Descent from the Cross*.

Master Konrad's style had exercised a wide influence, and the School of Westphalia had pentrated the adjacent regions as far as Thuringia and the Mark of Brandenburg when, in the second half of the fifteenth century, the supremacy passed from Soest to Münster, and the lessons of the Flemish became something approaching a tyranny among artists who lacked the powerful originality of Konrad von Soest to inspire them. The most remarkable among these Westphalian enthusiasts for the Flemish is Johann Körbecke (circa 1446-1491). The Amelsbüren *Crucifixion*, painted about 1450 (Münster) is his most significant work. For a long part of this period Körbecke was the only celebrated painter in Münster, but he trained pupils whose fame joined his own: Derik Baegert, who in 1494 painted the *Oath of the Judges* for the Townhall of Wesel where he lived; the two brothers Dünwege (Heinrich and Victor) in whom late Gothic realism blossomed out so brilliantly. The figures have a rough, powerful robustness; truth finds outward expression in gesture and almost in grimace; the wholly intimate art of the Westphalians of the first half of the century is becoming theatrical and slightly declamatory.

As for the Master of the *Liesborn Altarpiece* (painted in 1465), he earned the following eulogy from a contemporary humanist: "If he had lived among the Greeks, Pliny would have put him among the best masters of the liberal arts." A very active school developed round him [1].

NORTHERN GERMANY

JUST as it had happened in Westphalia, altarpiece painting which flourished in North Germany, and more especially in the Hanseatic towns of Hamburg and Lübeck, originates from the great mural decorations of the Romanesque and Gothic period, and there is something of these in the monumental sobriety of Master Bertram who, during the same period as Konrad von Soest, created the grand style of the German altarpiece.

Some art historians claim that Bertram (born circa 1345, no trace after 1415) was a native of Westphalia. He is supposed to have been born in Minden but we discover him settled in Hamburg in 1367, employed by the city to paint wooden statues which adorned the city gate. In 1375 he was sent off to Lübeck at the city's expense to join the school of local painters, and it was for the church of St. Peter in Hamburg, between the years 1379 and 1383, that he painted his masterpiece, the *Grabow Altar-piece* (Hamburg). As in the *Gold Altar-piece* of Lüneburg, the importance given to the gilded and polychromatic sculptural element obliged the artist to harmonize his panels with the plastic and spatial conception of the sculptor.

Master Bertram is, in the truest sense of the word, a narrator. Stories from the Scriptures and the life of Christ as he describes them in these twenty-four panels have a completely popular liveliness of expression and a vigorous and light hearted turn of wit. Master Bertram paints the objects which his personages use with naive satisfaction and even aims at tactile illusion, especially when he is dealing with wooden utensils. His conception of space is freer and more modern than Konrad's. Although he fixed his interior scenes by situating them under complicated and skilfully-worked baldachins, he is entirely indifferent to settings and attaches little importance to costume. His interest lies in truth of gesture, facial expression, the significant detail.

Some ten years later, in 1390, Bertram executed an altarpiece for the convent of Buxtehude, now known by that name (Hamburg). Although we now see a tendency to adopt the fashions of the Court of Burgundy in the more showy scenes, the all important element which distinguishes the Buxtehude from the Grabow altar-piece is a new feeling of a freer space and the advent of setting, that is, in the sense that the architectural element, confined for the most part to the baldachins in the Grabow altarpiece, now consists of an elaborate build-up of stage-flats, and there are, in addition, tentative hints of a natural background. It is a fact worth noticing, even if the painter's clumsiness and simplicity interfere with his interpretation of nature.

MASTER BERTRAM – THE CREATION OF THE ANIMALS. CIRCA 1380 – (0,86; 0,67) KUNSTHALLE, HAMBURG

Bertram's stay in Lübeck stimulated a lively artistic activity in that town in which so much of the Hanseatic wealth was concentrated.

In the hands of Master Francke, who lived in Hamburg during the first third of the fifteenth century, the eclecticism brought about by the interaction of the Westphalian and North German styles of painting resulted in works of splendid and fruitful originality such as the *St. Barbara Altarpiece*, in the National Museum of Helsinki and *the Englandfahrer Altar* or *St. Thomas à Becket*, in the Kunsthalle, Hamburg.

As opposed to Bertram, who was a prose-narrator, Francke is a poet; he is easily moved, and, effortlessly, in a lyrical, irrational atmosphere, he takes an obvious pleasure in reconstructing the order of things according to the whims and impulses of his imagination. A generation separates these two masters, but two entirely different conceptions of the universe inform their work. The characters are no longer rough-hewn, crudely dressed marionettes, but creatures of flesh and blood whose facial expressions reveal an intense personality. Bertram's attractive *gaucherie*

MASTER FRANCKE – THE SCOURGING. CIRCA 1425 – (0,99; 0,889) KUNSTHALLE, HAMBURG

becomes in Francke an opportunity for the display of a remarkable talent, especially in color, warm and flexible, in the play of light and shade, in which he exploits all the rich resources of chiaroscuro, even if it is still somewhat clumsy, and in his representation of the landscape which shows a wonderful combination of naturalist observation with visionary transposition.

Francke is at the same time a dramatist who stages the tragic episodes in the life of Thomas à Becket with dramatic violence and concentration. This almost expressionistic sense of the dramatic is something very novel in German painting of this period. Francke has furthermore a tender affection for inanimate objects and succeeds in expressing their density, weight and surface qualities with an entirely new sensibility. A similar tactile sense is observable in his expression of the landscape, with the stirring masses of the branches and the brown earth which clings to the fingers. Nature is alive in backgrounds of Francke's pictures, and the foliage seems to mingle with the lives of the characters. Perhaps the only other person in this period who managed to unify in this way the inanimate world with men's passions was the Swabian, Lucas Moser. For both of them direct expression produces a kind of "pastoral symphony," typically German in inspiration and character, which owes absolutely nothing to Flanders and Burgundy.

If Master Francke does not appear to have had any immediate followers pursuing the path he had opened up, Lübeck produced two very great artists, Hermen Rode and Bernt Notke, in the second half of the fifteenth century. Both worked in collaboration with sculptors, and Bernt Notke is, in point of fact, more famed for his sculpture than for his painting; his *St. George Slaying the Dragon*, in the Storkyrka at Stockholm, shows a visionary and savage vehemence which has perhaps no equivalent until the advent of Expressionism. The fact that we find his works as far afield as Esthonia and Denmark, is proof of the wide spread diffusion of Lübeck art in the Northern countries.

Hermen Rode (1468?-1504) is an admirable portraitist and a master of the intimate and the contemplative. The *St. Luke Altarpiece* which he painted in 1484 (Lübeck) has an intense, quiet sobriety. The peacefulness of closed rooms, discreetly lit, the profound truth of familiar objects — pots of paint in the St. Luke workshop look forward to Flegel, a hundred years before that German master of still life was active — strike a note that was unique in that period.

Bernt Notke was born at Ratzeburg in 1440 and he was given the title of master at Lübeck, the year that Rode was painting his first important picture, the altarpiece for the church of St. Nicholas at Stockholm (1468). He was to die in 1517 in the Swedish capital where he had settled in 1484, but it was at Lübeck that he painted his finest works, the *Aarhus Altarpiece*, for the Bishop of that Danish town, in 1479, and in 1483, for the mayor Hagenbecke, the *Altarpiece of the Church of the Holy Spirit* in Reval, Esthonia. Like the *Altarpiece of St. John* (1496, Lübeck), these two compositions reveal the sculptor as much as the painter in the vigorously emphasized three-dimensional quality, the weightiness of the characters and the striking, almost exaggerated relief in an expressive realism which borders on caricature.

BOHEMIA

THERE are striking analogies between the style of Master Bertram and that of a master whose sphere of influence extended far beyond the boundaries of Northern Germany to Bohemia and whom we know as Master Theodoric. Are we to infer a mutual influence, a double derivation from a common source or merely the fact that Theodoric was a German settled in Prague, round about the year 1350, working in the very Germanic atmosphere or the court of the two emperors, Charles IV and Wenceslas IV? The personality of both monarchs, men of international culture and strong individuality, can be recognized in the general character of the works executed in their reign, and one notices the change of the serious and monumental style of Master Theodoric to a courtly art which is reflected in the many examples of those Virgins, known under the appellation of "beautiful Madonnas".

We are not surprised to find in this art, as in any flourishing in an Imperial court, the eclecticism inseparable from the notion of empire. This does not mean that Bohemian painting of the fourteenth century lacks originality, far from it; but merely that, at this period, as later in the reign of Rudolph II, Prague was an international center of prodigious activity. The art of the various German schools, that of France, Italy and the Low Countries, combined harmoniously with national genius to create such homogeneity and unity that the masters of the period whose names are pretty vague, like Master Theodoric, or anonymous and known only under the designation of Master of Hohenfurth, Master of Wittingau, whatever country they haled from, represent a clearly defined element in the entity of European Gothic art. It was not until towards the end of the fourteenth century — as we discover from the guild registers — that the works of art were no longer preponderantly by German painters. There must have been an extraordinary profusion of paintings, judging only from the number of those that survive and which are themselves a tiny fraction of those examples that fell victims to Hussite iconoclasm. We know that in Prague alone existed sixty painted altarpieces in the cathedral, twenty-four in the church of Tyn and that the collegiate church of Vysehrad possessed thirty-two decorated altarpieces.

Open to every current influence, whether from Germany, France or Italy, Bohemia also welcomed a Byzantinism of Slav origin. Of this we can see an example in the paintings of the church of the Capucins of Prague in which the oriental *Deesis* is adorned with Czech ornaments while the rigid stylization of the bodies and faces is still preserved with a completely oriental soberness and austerity; and it is strange to notice that the line of the Mannerist and pre-Baroque "beautiful Madonnas" of the fourteenth century, is rounded off at the end of the century with the Madonna of Breznice (Prague), imitating a Roudnice ikon, reputed to have been painted by Saint Luke.

The first fourteenth century altarpiece painting, the *Roudnice Predella* (Prague), on the contrary, is the work of an artist who has evidently made a careful study of the Italian paintings, imported in great numbers, and consciously imitated no less in miniatures than in altar pictures. According to Matejcek and Pesina, Bohemia was of all European countries in the fourteenth century the one where Gothic painting was the most strongly influenced by elements from the Italian Peninsula.

Happily the native painters and the German immigrants in Prague opposed these Italianizing tendencies with their own vigorous originality. The most strange and original of the Czech artists of the mid-fourteenth century, Master Theodoric, has an expressionistic realism all his own, the finest and most impressive manifestation of which is the remarkably well preserved ensemble of the Chapel of the Holy Cross in Burg Karlstein. These innumerable effigies of saints, evangelists, popes and kings, sitting side by side as in a portrait gallery, have as their distinguishing

THE MASTER OF THE WITTINGAU ALTAR – THE RESURRECTION. CIRCA 1380 – (1,32; 0,92) NATIONAL GALLERY, PRAGUE

mark the exclusive importance the artist has given to the human face. He accentuates almost savagely the solid, tangible, semi-illusionist humanity of these large, massive heads which have a peasant roughness and are for the most part devoid of any spiritual element. The enormous vitality of the facial expressions links Master Theodoric, whether he be of German origin or not, with the constant of the Faustian portrait which combines the element of what a character is destined to *become* with what he actually *is*; of this we shall have more to say later. His realism goes so far as to endow his *St. Maurice* of Burg Karlstein with all the ethnological characteristics of the negro, with an accent of truth that is near caricature in its expressiveness. This in fact is one of the traits common to several painters of this period who were inspired by Master Theodoric, or even working in his circle, for whom the importance of realism is the prerequisite of a work of art.

A painting style never comes to a sudden stop. If Master Theodoric's genius had for several decades swept aside Italian influences and the ideals of Czech painting and had isolated his pupils and direct imitators, he nevertheless left no permanent following. Expressionist naturalism in its turn was attacked by a kind of Franco-germanic eclecticism in which Theodoric's essentially Czech temperament was attenuated and finally banished. The works of the Master of Wittingau, who was active about 1380, mark a frank and lively reaction of spirituality against Mannerism and a retreat from realistic portraiture in favor of landscape and space, which was beginning to become a plastic preoccupation at that time. The linear rhythms of drapery, the elongation of the human figure, in accordance with the Gothic canon, nervous and sensitive draughtsmanship replace the muscular, not to say adipose heaviness of the Karlstein saints.

The *Wittingau Altarpiece* (at present in the National Gallery of Prague) which gives the anonymous master his name, was painted about 1380 for the Augustinian monastery of Wittingau. Its creator was both a mystic and a man of the theatre, admirable at exploiting the dramatic side of a scene like the Resurrection, with its red sky sprinkled with golden stars, an unreal background such as we find again in the Garden of Olives, with the supple and undulating lines of the bodies, the trance-like beauty of the faces, the visionary violence of the concentrated composition. In the hands of the Master of Wittingau, space becomes an emotional factor to be reckoned with, and light itself evokes a world beyond this palpable earth, an inner pathos for whose composite sources we must look to Germany, France and the Low Countries. Czech Gothic reaches its climax in this *Wittingau Altarpiece.*

If Master Theodoric sometimes makes one think back to Bertram and the North Germans, the Master of Wittingau would appear to have more affinities with Westphalia and even Cologne, but Burgundy and Bruges also contributed a different element, a composite one, which, without having any detrimental effect on the sturdy originality of this painter, prove him to be a much less localized eclectic than the Master of Burg Karlstein; and it is an analogous ecleticism that we encounter among the artists who worked in the Master of Wittingau's entourage, or, at any rate, in his style[2].

The multiplicity of Madonnas that occur in Czech painting in the fourteenth and fifteenth centuries arises from the importance which the Marian cult had assumed before the advent of the Hussites. The book of John of Streda, the apostolate of

Archbishop Arnost of Pardubice, Charles IV's councillor, who is known to have commissioned a great many images of Our Lady and recommended that prayers to the Blessed Virgin should be translated into German and Czech so that they should gain a wider popularity, explain much better than the early vogue for Italian Madonnas why Bohemia produced an infinite number of extremely varied paintings during this period. The Byzantine-influenced Peribleptos of Roudnice is an exception; the general run consists of what have been familiarly called the "beautiful Madonnas" — tender, elegant, sentimental, often extremely mannered, which, because of these reasons, exercised a greater influence on popular sensibility [3].

The beginnings of the fifteenth century saw the growth of that Baroque spirit associated with the "beautiful Madonnas" which is something more than the mannerism of dying Gothic and almost a foretaste of what real Baroque was to be in the seventeenth century, in a Bohemia already so well prepared to receive it. The Marian cult of John of Streda and Arnost of Pardubice develops in the direction of a more fleshly not to say almost worldly beauty, derived from the art of the Wenceslas court.

After 1470, Czech religious art went back more and more to the aesthetic principles of the German schools and found a more sustaining nourishment particularly in the robust and somewhat crude sobriety of the Franconians. Unfortunately the deposition of Wenceslas in 1411 had already dealt a harsh blow at the artistic prosperity of Prague, and Hussite troubles were to precipitate disorder and savage destruction, with fatal results for Czech art; Bohemia was never again to see that uninhibited efflorescence of a genuine national art, the product of a fruitful and enchanting eclecticism. The artists emigrated in great numbers to Germany, the home of their ancestors or masters in the previous century.

FRANCONIA

During the second half of the fourteenth and beginning of the fifteenth century at any rate, the development of Franconia is to some extent linked up with that of Bohemia through the choice of Nuremberg as twin capital, co-equal with Prague, by Charles IV and his son Wenceslas. Both towns, in which the sovereign resided alternately, were therefore able to establish a continual interchange of artistic ideas. The evidence of this traffic can be seen in the great mural decorations, and the easel-paintings such as the *Imhoff Altarpiece* in the church of St. Lawrence in Nuremberg. This altar is attributed to a very little-known master, called Bertholt Landauer, but it could equally well be an extension of the "circle" of the Master of Wittingau, so much do certain details of treatment and even the central idea of the construction remind us of Prague. Painted in all probability about the year 1420, the *Imhoff Altarpiece* still comes within the orbit of Czech influence, but this eclecticism was soon to vanish from the school of Nuremberg, although we continue to notice borrowings from Italian painting in the Bamberg Altarpiece (Bayerisches Museum, Munich).

The *Tucher Altarpiece*, on the other hand, painted about twenty years later (the Church of Our Lady, Nuremberg), is strongly imbued with a vigor that seems to have deserted Czech Gothic of the same period. We note a great contrast between the short, squat figures, of a peasant cast of feature, and the gold, diapered background with its elaborate pendentives under Gothic pinnacles. Renaissance realism is here associated with medieval idealism in an extremely attractive combination. And it is precisely these qualities that we are to discover in another contemporary work, the *Altarpiece* styled *"Of the Mediators,"* by an unknown painter whose presence was recorded at Nuremberg between 1430 and 1445. The Altar which lends its name to this anonymous master (Church of the Holy Cross, Nuremberg) and the three panels of the Altar of St. Catherine, preserved in the Alte Pinakothek in Munich, are of a subtler art than the Tucher Altar, more open to charm and fantasy; landscape elements are set against the gold background, discreetly, it is true, but they suffice to voice that wealth of emotion, arising from contact with nature, expressed in the harmonious evocation of mountains and valleys, familiar to us in the *Altarpiece of the Augustinians*, formerly known as the *Peringsdörffer Altarpiece* (circa 1487, Nuremberg). If the *Saint Luke painting the Madonna* shows an intense love of intimate detail, akin to that of Flemish painting, the *Vision of Saint Bernard* already possesses the dramatic power and almost the visionary realism that we are to encounter later in Matthias Grünewald.

Hitherto in the Franconian school we have encountered only anonymous, if highly individualized painters, but with Hans Pleydenwurff (active 1457-1472) we meet a completely identifiable and authenticated person to whom we are doubly indebted for some remarkable works and also for the considerable part he played in the education and aesthetic development of the young Dürer. He is thought to have been born about 1420 in Bamberg, but it is not known where he learned his craft nor who were his masters. The Munich *Crucifixion* dates from the period of his full maturity. He had long since put his apprenticeship, which he is believed to have spent in the Low Countries, behind him. Although he was not strictly speaking a cosmopolitan, his eclecticism of technique caused him to be appreciated far beyond the confines of Franconia and summoned to countries as far distant as Silesia and Poland to carry out important commissions.

The figure of Christ in the Munich *Crucifixion* is reminiscent of the Augustinian Altarpiece (formerly attributed to the hypothetical Wolgemut) but the landscape which occurs in the background is certainly in the Flemish manner, with its miniaturist narrative of distant cities; and the attitudes, the facial expressions are full of memories of Roger van der Weyden. Pleydenwurff's outstanding merit is that, in spite or even because of this plagiarism, he created the Franconian style which escapes the limitations of provincial schools and, instead of being circumscribed within a frozen technique and aesthetic system, remains open to the lessons of foreign masters.

The *Hof Altarpiece* was formerly attributed to Michael Wolgemut, about whom the tradition runs that he had married the widow of Pleydenwurff, his master. Present day criticism tends to reverse the proportion of the merits once acknowledged to master and pupil. If it is difficult to discriminate when dealing with work emanating from a studio between Pleydenwurff's, his son Wilhelm's and even young Dürer's share — for Dürer was one of the apprentices in the *bottega* — the modern tendency is to belittle Wolgemut's talent in favor of his master. Hence a masterpiece of the greatest importance like the *Hof Altarpiece* (dated 1465, Munich) is now attributed to Pleydenwurff himself whose idiom and personality are better known. There is more verve, simple grandeur and sober lyricism in this polyptych than in paintings that can be assigned with certainty to Wolgemut, such as the *Zwickau Nativity* (1479), very different in its general spirit and details from what Pleydenwurff has painted.

The argument concerning these two major Franconian painters is too complex to enter into here. It is moreover only of moderate interest, but the previous tendency to overestimate the importance of Wolgemut carries the risk of making us unjust towards him, now that his activity and artistic claims are so much minimized. In a period when the work in a studio involved a certain unity of style and the strong stamp of the dominating personalities, the problem of attributions is bound to present difficulties.

SWABIA

Rich trading cities in which the merchant class reconciles a taste for money with a love of culture; a fertile, somewhat wild country, imbuing its inhabitants with a sense of practical, everyday, not to say "terre-à-terre" reality. And these people with their healthy, vigorous and solid physique have their feet firmly planted on the soil. Even the spiritual element has too much grossness. The figures in Swabian paintings of the fifteenth century, with their virile, almost peasant robustness, embody the essential characteristics of a country which was to prove one of the most fertile in original talents. The whole corpus of Swabian painting during that and the succeeding century, is distinguished by this realism, untinged with vulgarity, this sense of the picturesque which always keeps close to everyday life. We must insist however that, although this notion of "school" is given some prominence in discussing art in the Germany of this period, the term bears neither a limiting nor exclusive connotation. Rarely, in fact, have artists moved about so much, and we might compare the German Schools to what is nowadays known as the "School of Paris", since artists haled from a diversity of German states, eager to settle in large art centers. The result was that regional peculiarities abounded and enriched other soils, and a certain eclecticism was established which gave freedom and diversity to the basic characteristics of each province.

We note, for example that in Swabia, the first seascape was painted, in 1431, by an artist from Würtemberg, Lukas Moser, on the altarpiece of a parish church at Tiefenbronn, near Pforzheim, and not, as we might expect in Hamburg or Lübeck. The *Altarpiece of Saint Magdalene* at Tiefenbronn provides us with the most interesting date in the art of this first half of the fifteenth century. The features of the painting in question are strikingly modern but the inscription which accompanies it reveals a disillusionment and sense of discouragement in Lukas Moser, as if he was conscious of losing the favor of his public which was attracted by a newer aesthetic creed "Schri, Kunst, schri und klag dich ser, dein begert jetz niemer mer, so o we." Which

LUKAS MOSER – THE PASSAGE OF THE SAINTS, 1431 – RIGHT-HAND SHUTTER (1,49; 0,59) ALTARPIECE IN THE CHURCH OF TIEFENBRONN

can be roughly translated thus: "Cry, O art, and bewail, for no one, alas, will have any more of you now!".

The most arresting elements of a moving novelty however are present in this calm yet vigorous work. The love of reality is expressed in each almost "documentary" detail of the techniques of the period — the portable table for supper in the garden of the *Supper with Lazarus*, the rigging of the ships sailing on Lake Constance, stylized to represent the Mediterranean, the lozenge-shaped tiles on the shutters. It would be a waste of time to look for the atmosphere of the miracle, the *aura* of the supernatural in this precise but not over-detailed objectivity, which the artist's deep love for the humble objects of everyday life transmutes into poetry. At the same time we become aware that Lukas Moser solved the problem of situating man on space without aiming, however, at verisimilitude and exact relationships between people and inanimate objects. The five sailors have embarked in a tiny skiff which would hardly do for one, and in his buildings there is such a lack of space that the people squeeze, uncomfortably, as best they can, into a room hardly bigger than a cupboard.

Any objection on this score would be meaningless to Lukas Moser, for reality is a very different thing from a lazy conformity with such purely accidental relationships. The truth about people and objects is in the aspect they present, in the ripple of the tiny waves which express the joyful movement of the sea, in the green transparency of the water through which you can see the ship's hull, in the healthy, appetizing smell of whole-meal bread set out on the tables. Therein lies Lukas Moser's greatness; therein we see, from the first third of the fifteenth century, the growth of that conception of life and art peculiar to Swabian painters and to which Conrad Witz, substituting vigor for elegance, was to add his own characteristic peaceful and smiling dignity and squat monumentality.

KONRAD WITZ

THE ROMAN IDEALISM (Gantner) of the painter of *The Miraculous Draught of Fishes* has its origin in the same aesthetic principles which guided Lukas Moser; we must not forget the considerable influence of the Council of Basle on the artists of the first half of the fifteenth century, since it brought together the artists and scholars who accompanied the churchmen on their journeys and the statesmen who took part in it. Italy was to some extent in advance of Germany and the eclecticism of national or provincial schools profited by the fact.

The slight information we have about the life of Konrad Witz up to his arrival at Basle about 1430 tells us nothing of his birth place (Constance or Rottweil?), his parentage (his father might be the Hans of Constance who worked for Philip the Good); but we may suppose that he was brought up in the ambience of Swabian realism, the characteristics of which are to be seen in his work. But it is to Basle where he settled, received the freedom of the city in 1435 and died a decade later, that he belongs. It is thought that his masters may have been Niklaus Lawlin Rüsch, a Swabian settled in Basle and painter of the *Crucifixion of the Chartreuse* (dated 1438), who had been living in Basle since 1405; and a native of Alsace, Hans Tieffenthal of Sélestat, who was a painter in Basle in 1422. In his monumental realism, the pondered and interrogative gravity of the countenances, the peasant simplicity of the heavy bodies, contrasting with the solemnity of the sacred subject, in his modest fidelity to the material of inanimate objects — the wood of the door, the rough cast of the wall, the parchment of a binding — no less than in the gentle steadfastness of an angel's gaze (*Annunciation*, Nuremberg), Witz is almost a realist. Much more, however, he is a painter preoccupied above all with the relationship between the human figure and the surrounding space, the quality of the atmosphere that circulated round the bodies, the shadows which play on the walls and flag stones, the reflections on the curvature of a piece of armor, the pommel of a sword.

In his feeling for space and the problems of its expression and representation, he is expert in the highest degree, but he retains the ingenuousness of the popular story teller who is amused by the piquant details of his narrative: the *Altarpiece of Saint Peter*, painted after 1443 for the Bishop of Geneva, François de Mez (Geneva), is an extremely simple altarpiece; we note however that, more in this example than in the *Altarpiece of the Mirror of Salvation*, painted circa 1435, the panels of which are now dispersed in various museums, — the greatest number being in Basle — Witz stands out from his contemporaries, as Gantner has emphasized, in that, unlike them, he is not a narrative realist "but a realist of solemn, hieratic figures and groups of figures." A bare ten to fifteen years divide the *Tiefenbronn Altarpiece* from the *Altarpiece of Saint Peter*, but there is a whole world between Lukas Moser and Konrad Witz. The landscape with Lake Geneva and the distant mountains has been praised too often for the eulogy to be repeated here, but the way the "ghost" of the resurrected Christ *is present* in this natural and unpretentious landscape which combines the supernatural with the real, was within the power alone of Konrad Witz to express with such shattering intensity. The gesture by which the Angel seizes hold of the wrist of a Saint Peter still sleepy and bewildered by the event, to lead him out of his prison, is of a modest yet profound humanity, perhaps beyond the capacity of any of Witz' contemporaries, for the artists of the Cologne School would have probably introduced a theatrical touch of which there is no trace here.

HANS MULTSCHER

This theatricality of attitudes, of expressions shading into grimaces, of gestures that turn into gesticulations, is not necessarily, as is sometimes supposed, an admission of the absence of a true inner life, but rather of a lack of power to express it except in ponderously materialistic terms. Multscher indeed reminds us of those amateur actors of Mystery plays, those artisan actors at whom Shakespeare pokes fun, who believed that excessive mime compensated for a lack of professionalism that is based on restraint and aims at absolute simplicity. Once his emotions come into play, Multscher grimaces and gesticulates, but it because his ebullient and almost athletic temperament demands an outlet. Yet it is he who supplies the foundation

KONRAD WITZ – THE DELIVERANCE OF ST. PETER. 1444 – (1,32; 1,54)
THE MUSEUM OF ART AND HISTORY, GENEVA

of the whole Swabian school of the fifteenth and sixteenth centuries, and his very faults appear meritorious since they have had such fruitful results. Engraver, painter, sculptor, accustomed to brushing in those vast altarpieces which adorn the churches of Ulm, Augsburg, Nördlingen and some of which were exported to other German states, Multscher is more an exponent of the last phase of Gothic art than a "modern" like Witz. A native of Würtemberg, born about the year 1400 at Reichenhofen near Leutkirch, he was already a burgher of Ulm by 1427 and was destined to live there another forty years of uninterrupted activity. Proof of this are many works of undisputed authenticity and others which may well be from his hands.

The eight panels of a large altarpiece — the central panel is lost — which are in Berlin (1437) reveal Multscher in his rather brutal and somewhat primitive strength; for him expression is of paramount importance; to it he subordinates all formal problems and any idea of style. Muscular effort, the twitchings of the face mean more to him than the truth of the relationship between man and the surrounding objects; *Pentecost* and *The Death of the Virgin* take place in a room whose dimensions do not exceed those of a cupboard, and sometimes he is so clumsy in expressing his gestures that the suffering of Christ looks more like anger. In the *Resurrection*, however, he shows Christ, flesh and bone though he is, passing through the heavy lid of the tomb. Here Multscher's aptitude for depicting the supernatural in the very midst of the solid and earthly obliges us to reject the reproach that is sometimes brought against him of being prosaic and banal. Whatever means he employs, the expression, successful and complete or not, that he strives to achieve is his one and only concern.

This wildly concentrated grandeur is unfortunately lacking in a Swabian artist, the Master of the Sterzing Altar (1458), who knew Multscher and probably collaborated with him. He is more sober, elegant, modern, it is true, in the sense that he has none of Multscher's medieval grossness. The aesthetic development of Ulm and Augsburg, possibly under the influence of the Flemish whose work was eagerly sought after by the wealthy merchant class and financiers, moved away from Multscher's expressionism.

The Altarpiece painted by Hans Schüchlin in 1469 for the same church of Tiefenbronn where Lukas Moser's altarpiece was already *in situ*, shows a striving after elegance, a modest sobriety which is not really Flemish and might be said to have more affinity with the Franconian school, with Wolgemut perhaps and with the *Hofer Altarpiece* (Munich 1465). Schüchlin was born in Ulm and died there in 1505, but nothing is known about his travels and what painter he worked with.

We must look to Nuremberg for the genesis of style which belongs in part, at any rate, to Friedrich Herlin (circa 1459-1500). Herlin belongs to a Swabian background, if not by birth, at least in his training. A native of Rothenburg, he worked at Nördlingen which must be considered his real artistic home ground. The wings of the Altarpiece of the church of St. George, Nördlingen (1488) lead us to infer that he must have known Roger van der Weyden, but in certain intimate details of charming picturesqueness — the model ship hanging above the door in the Pharisee's house — we recognize an almost comic realism which is very typical of him. This aspect of his painting influenced Bartholomaüs Zeitblom who, before entering the workshop of Schüchlin whose daughter he married, was Herlin's pupil.

Zeitblom himself died in 1517; he was familiar with the work of Dürer and imitated his style of engraving. All the same it is with Zeitblom that the Swabian school reaches its eclectic grandeur, its classic beauty before taking a Baroque turn in the hands of Burgkmair, Ulrich Apt and Holbein the Elder whose work bore the stamp of Italian influence. Zeitblom had none of this, but in his depictions of the life and miracles of St. Valentine (Augsburg), who was the Bishop of Interamnum, the figures have a static severity, as if they were petrified, and we notice the same feature in the panels of the *Eschach Altarpiece* (1496) which has an Annunciation, charming in its discretion, reserve and intensity.

The discovery of Italy, in the north of which this artist made the traditional tour of technical and aesthetic training round about his twentieth year, and the sight of works by Mantegna, Donatello, the Bellinis and the different approach of Italian artists to plastic problems and, above all, that of the representation of space, raised, in the person of Michael Pacher, the somewhat provincial art of this family of painters and sculptors, certainly of painter-sculptors too, which had settled in the Pustertal and was, in the work of Friedrich Pacher (born circa 1440) already acquiring a justifiable fame[5], to a kind of attractive and grandiose syncretism.

Michael Pacher's genius and renown have overshadowed the still rustic and not altogether successful idiom of Friedrich; it would however be unjust to neglect what the former owes to him in his early training and the extent to which the Pacher idiom shows a family likeness that implies a close collaboration and studio work in common among the members of this family and artistic community. This would account for the admirable homogeneity we find in the painted and sculpted elements revealed with trembling majesty in the *St. Wolfgang Altarpiece.*

If we accept Michael Pacher's date of birth as 1435, he would have been thirty-six at the time when he was given two important commissions, the *Altarpiece of Gries* and the winged altar of *St. Wolfgang.* Of the former little survives and we must visit St. Wolfgang if we are to study a fifteenth-century altarpiece in all its plastic, symbolic and theological articulation and analyse the essential characteristics of Michael Pacher. It is an art that has retained an atmosphere of the mountains and if the rural nature of the squat figures of Friedrich give way to a suppler and slighter physique, a certain angular stiffness shows traces of an archaism that lingers on in the very midst of this modern revolution.

We are bound in fact to salute one of the most "modern" artists of his time in this painter of St. Wolfgang who resolves the most complex spatial problems with calm audacity. Whenever an opportunity occurs for constructing a space in which buildings fit naturally and harmoniously into a newly-devised system of perspective according to the particular problem and in which monumental figures move with the serene solemnity of men in harmony with the atmosphere they breathe and the soil they tread, Michael Pacher combines his recollections of Italy with a valid and individual solution. This solution possesses a three-dimensional quality full of the breath of life, and the artist preserves, moreover, a fresh ingenuousness in the choice and use of picturesque detail from the Gothic heritage which he never entirely repudiated. The Venetian grace which he has assimilated softens and illumines the faces of the sacred characters with a ray of glowing spirituality, and this, together with the warm and brilliant coloring, makes you think of the lesson that some Netherland artist has learned directly from, or through the intermediary of Italy.

His gift for recounting a story with zest is finely balanced with the plastic feeling which remains the dominant passion of a painter who practised painting among sculptors and probably did some sculpture himself — so great is the analogy, so close the homogeneity between the carved and painted parts of the *St. Wolfgang Altar* — but who at any moment is able to make an eminently plastic solution also an eminent-

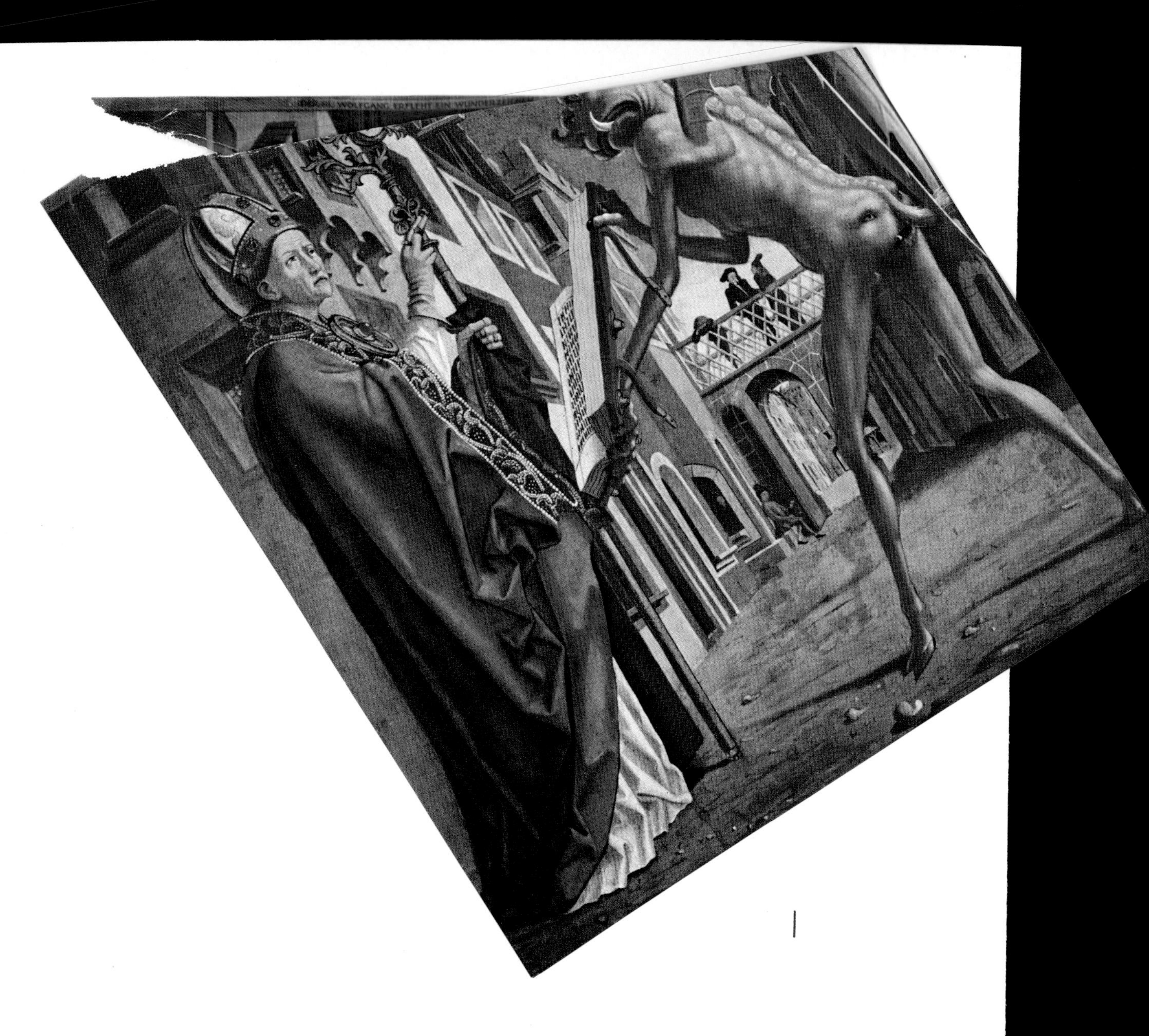

MICHAEL PACHER – ST. WOLFGANG FORCES THE DEVIL TO HOLD THE PRAYER BOOK FOR HIM 1486-1490 – (1,03; 0,91) ALTE PINAKOTHEK, MUNICH

ly pictorial one. This is particularly evident in the *Altarpiece of the Fathers of the Church* (painted between 1486 and 1490 for the Collegiate church at Neustift, at present in the Alte Pinakothek, Munich) in which the fantastic expression of the supernatural — in the conversation between the Devil and St. Wolfgang, for example — strangely combines the goat-like legs of Pan with a face and torso borrowed from the medieval hell, direct legacies from the carnival masks in mountain villages with their pagan flavor and the property shop of the Mystery plays.

More modern in his feeling for plastic form than in his manner of telling a story, Michael Pacher effortlessly achieves a monumentality in his isolated figures which makes a strange contrast with the architecture of the Gothic setting. His landscapes are conventional except when he borrows the majestic wooded slopes, delicately sinuous stretches of water and the idyllic life of the animals that walk in the

FRIEDRICH HERLIN – WOMEN PRAYING. 1488 – (0,90; 0,67) CITY MUSEUM, NÖRDLINGEN

forest from the Mondsee valley where the parish church of St. Wolfgang stands. Not too well equipped for endowing human faces with the deep emotions that animate them, he nevertheless rejects those eloquent grimaces which his predecessors indulged in to convey terrible suffering and extreme bliss. In a static marmorean impassivity in the pure Mantegna tradition, he tacitly admits the difficulty he finds in conveying emotions in facial expression.

It was natural that so new, energetic and fascinating an idiom as that of Michael Pacher's should find disciples, not only in the family circle — his brother Hans of whom little is known collaborated with him — but also affect the whole corpus of Austrian art extending as far as Bavaria[5].

More distant still and less defined is the influence it may well have exercised on aesthetic centers geographically and aesthetically remote, such as the Danube School and on Wolf Huber, a native of Vorarlberg, who is thought to have been born in Feldkirch about 1490 but spent the years from 1515 when he arrived during his childhood to his death in 1553, in Passau. Huber is a wonderful draughtsman, adept at interpreting the dramatic moods of a nature that is now idyllically calm, now convulsively roused into perpetual effervescence by the superabundance of cosmic sap. It is this trait which has so long caused him to be associated in people's minds with Altdorfer whose pupil he is thought to have been. When one examines the landscape which serves as a background to his famous *Portrait of Jacob Ziegler* (Vienna), one realizes how rare and original such sensibility to nature is, and that Huber opens the way to an almost Impressionist conception, nearer to the Mondsee landscape which Pacher painted in the St. Wolfgang panel depicting the saint building the walls of his church than the visionary pantheism of Altdorfer's *Battle of Arbela* or the *St. George*.

The part played by Wolf Huber in this discovery of landscape, one of the most felicitous and fruitful conquests of German painting in the sixteenth century, is as personal, as freely and vigorously individualized as the landscape idiom of Dürer, Matthias Grünewald, Altdorfer, Hans Baldung or Cranach. His human type is more expansive, subtler, more fleshly than Michael Pacher's.

Between Michael Pacher, from whom he clearly derives, and Altdorfer whom he must have been aware of in his early days, stands a no less remarkable Austrian master, Marx Reichlich. An inhabitant, if not a native of Salzburg (he appeared there in 1494, was elected a citizen and died in 1520), Reichlich continued the Expressionist vein of Pacher. He has a predilection for fantastic lighting effects, chiaroscuro of a highly accentuated tragic intensity; he did not hesitate to make his executioners' faces grimace with hatred, or show his martyrs' features distorted with agony. He treats the landscape with a sober realism and breaks up the architectural structure with arbitrary foreshortening. He is capable, however, of being more classically Italianate than Pacher, although he had not perhaps any first hand knowledge of Mantegna or Giovanni Bellini. The panels of his *Life of the Virgin*, now dispersed, show a conception of more "open" space than Michael Pacher's, more diversified in its perspective articulations. One is struck by the curious, rising perspective of his *Crowning with Thorns* (Munich) in which the streets, seen through the narrow window, force the houses to climb one above the other, for lack of space, improbably as in the décor of a German Expressionist film.

RUELAND FRUEAUF THE YOUNGER – ST. LEOPOLD GOES HUNTING. 1507 – (0,76; 0,39) STIFTSMUSEUM, KLOSTERNEUBURG

Bavaria did not come forward as an autonomous artistic province. Bavarian art of the fifteenth century is scarcely distinguishable from Austrian art of the same period.

Jan Pollack, who died in 1519[6], followed Pacher's lead with regard to conception of space and the three-dimensional quality of his figures; but at the same time he is more outwardly dramatic and decorative in the sense that he is fond of architectural ornaments, anecdotal details; his chief merit is his ability to relate a story with verve and pathos which holds the spectator breathless, as, for example, in the scenes depicting the false miracles of *Simon Magus.*

Rueland Frueauf the Younger (circa 1470-1545), although initiated into the ideas of the Italian Renaissance, remains closer to his father, Rueland Frueauf the Elder (circa 1445-1507) than Pacher. This can be seen even in the construction of the landscape of *the Altarpiece of St. Leopold* (the Abbey at Klosterneuburg, 1507), almost stylized in the spirit of the fifteenth century to which he belongs only by the first part of his life.

THE SCHOOL OF COLOGNE

We must guard against an indiscriminate acceptance of the usual hackneyed pronouncements on the dreamy tenderness of the Masters of the School of Cologne, their distinguished delicacy and aristocratic elegance. Lochner's example weighed heavily on the aesthetic evolution of his fellow citizens in all conscience, but if in the School as a whole we recognize a family likeness that justifies the name of "School ", we cannot neglect the compelling interest, observable in the strong and authentic originality of those anonymous Masters who go under the names of the Master of St. Severin, the Master of the Legend of St. Ursula, the Master of the Bartholomew Altarpiece, the Master of the Legend of St. George, about all of whose lives we know nothing, but who reveal their personality and authority in a remarkable fashion.

In its beginnings, the art of Cologne was closely bound up with the Gothic aesthetic system, its precise, somewhat prosaically decorative drawing, abstract, gold backgrounds, calligraphic silhouettes, to be found in a host of large and small polyptychs that fill churches and monasteries; and of these there was no lack in the "City of the Ten Thousand Virgins." The hypothetical Master Wilhelm, who may have been Wilhelm von Herle (circa 1358-1378), and Hermann Wynrich in the employ of the Dukes of Burgundy in the first quarter of the fifteenth century are credited — if not very convincingly — with a large number of these anonymous works in which there is more than a hint of the individuality of the Master of St. Veronica, the Master of the Claren Altarpiece (Cologne), and the Master of the Berlin Triptych.

An extremely refined, "courtly" style — in the sense that we speak of "courtly" love — that recalls the poetry of the Minnesinger and mediaeval romances of chivalry, lends this pre-Lochner production a suave and pensive devotional air, combined with a delicate and dignified worldliness and almost childlike candor. The

THE MASTER OF ST. VERONICA – ARRIVAL OF ST. URSULA AT COLOGNE (DETAIL). CIRCA 1411-1414 – (0,60; 1,79)
WALLRAF-RICHARTZ MUSEUM, COLOGNE

attitudes, gestures and expressions are dominated by a certain formalism. It is the mannerism of late Gothic which stylizes the emotions, the movements of the body and impulses of the mind in a kind of refined theatricality which rejects naturalism for a dreamy unreality, an almost childish conception of an earth and heaven in which everything takes place in accordance with pleasant conventions and exquisite modes of behavior, thought and feeling.

Stefan Lochner (1400-1451) is distinguishable from the general run of his compatriots only by his feeling for nature, closer to reality and less fanciful than theirs. In him we find much of that hedonism which in the *Dombild* of Cologne Cathedral, the Altenburg *Nativity* and the *Presentation of the Child Christ in the Temple* at Darmstadt (1447) perpetuates the convention of an idyllic world in which the Magi and saintly knights look like children dressed up for some civic festival. Although this grace is very spontaneous and unaffected, and the luxury of the costumes, jewelry and the splendor of the weapons merely emphasize the display element, so beloved of the Cologne citizens at this period, and although Lochner is evidently reacting against the influence of the Flemish who were in direct contact with the Rhineland and attracted the connoisseurs of the time, one still feels tempted to criticize this art for the very excess of its qualities — the abuse of the exquisite.

Lochner is not *the* great painter who roused the enthusiasm of the Romantics when they "discovered" medieval art in a cartload of triptychs of the fourteenth and fifteenth centuries which was about to be used for firewood; he belongs to a Middle Ages which had become conventional like opera, insipid, not to say anemic, through too much civilization, refinement and charm. No one would deny that he is *a* great painter, responsible as he was for introducing a new sensibility, modernizing his predecessors' archaisms, transposing and acclimatizing the style of the Low Countries. In this way he helped his contemporaries and successors to liberate themselves both from the influence he himself exercised, by offsetting it with that of the Flemish, and in digesting this influence which he integrated into the old German tradition. Thanks to him, the anonymous masters of the fifteenth century enlarged their plastic vocabulary, warmed up their palettes, renewed their vision of the world. Instead of pupils inspired by a "School" spirit, therefore, we have frank and vigorous individuals following in his wake.

What counts above all with these great Cologne masters of the fifteenth century is not so much their resemblances as their differences; each one possesses his own genuine and personal merits — the Master of the Legend of St. George (Cologne), a feeling for landscape that shows an ingenuous but true sensibility; the Master of the Passion of Lyversberg, the sincerity of facial expression and gestures, a monumental calm, a contained grief, decreed by the spiritual power which controls the whole architecture of the composition and makes the colors sing like the voices in a Bach chorale. In the Master of the Life of the Virgin we recognize the art of disposing the figures and setting them in motion in a lighter, more vibrant air, an open wind-swept space; if the Master of the Holy Family displays a predilection for the brilliance of ceremonial vestments, golds, brocades and delicate, flamboyant buildings (the Altar of St. Sebastian, 1493; Family Altar of Gumprecht von Neuenjahr, 1485, Cologne), he achieves it with an easy and happy grace that, on occasion, already gives us a foretaste of the Renaissance.

In the same way we are already conscious of the almost quivering sensibility, sometimes Burgundian in form but almost Baroque in spirit, in the movement of the garments, the exaggerated melodrama of the expressions, the violence of the rhythmic currents which sweep through a monumental work such as the Altarpiece of St. Thomas (Cologne, circa 1499), by that Master of the Bartholomew Altarpiece (circa 1470-1510) who already takes us to the brink of the sixteenth century. He is an earthy painter, intoxicated with fleshly beauty, not in the mannered way of the Flemish, of whom the Master of the Glorification of the Virgin is more reminiscent. In his strange treatment of faces, elongated, bathed in a cold light, the Master of St. Severinus displays an intentional, emphasized realism that runs counter to every kind of formalism and stylization.

Taken as a whole, the Cologne School of the fifteenth century is in revolt against national traditions and even against the foreign influences which it contrives to exploit without any sacrifice of its own personality. Thus the Master of the Legend of St. Ursula, who was active about the end of the fifteenth century, harmoniously combines an Italian lightness with the attractive color of the Flemish, and yet he does not fail to transmute all these ingredients with a power derived from his equal infatuation for the natural and the supernatural. In the *Legend of St. Ursula* we have none of those archaic constructions still beloved of the Master of St. Veronica and the Master of the Glorification of Mary; but the artist has had the temerity to cut into the gold background against which the saints of his Stadtbild (Cologne, end of fifteenth century) are silhouetted, to make room for a panorama of his native

THE MASTER OF ST. URSULA – THE ANGEL APPEARS TO ST. URSULA. CIRCA 1500 – (1,23; 1,14) WALLRAF-RICHARTZ MUSEUM, COLOGNE

city and the Siebengebirge, interesting because of its documentary detail and as a contribution to the new direction which landscape is taking.

The artistic development achieved on every side by the Cologne painters, starting from the hypothetical Master Wilhelm and his entourage of anonymous masters of the fourteenth century, stimulated by Lochner who, we must not forget, is the creator of the grandiose *Last Judgment,* the center panel of a scattered triptych (Cologne, Munich, Frankfurt) which is far from owing everything to the Flemish, opening out fan-like in the vigorous variety of innumerable original masters of the fifteenth century, ends up with a distinguished eclectic such as the Master of the Aix-la-Chapelle Altarpiece (*Adoration of the Magi*, Berlin, early sixteenth century) who has broken away from the Low Countries. Cologne is now turning rather towards Swabia or Franconia.

It is the period when a composite style was being evolved, the different elements of which offset, not to say, cancel out each other; thus, powerful personalities, genuinely new talents find favor. How are we to classify these eclectics? Anton Wonsam came from Worms (circa 1500-1541), but all his active life was spent in Cologne, and it is in the development of that School that he takes his place as an extremely important climax (*Crucifixion*, Budapest) in which painter and engraver come to terms in an extraordinary way. The Master of the Passion of Darmstadt is a recluse, a sober, extremely introspective artist who rejects every useless ornament; his *Holy Trinity* in Berlin, no less than the *Darmstadt Altarpiece* from which he takes his name, is a fine example of that economy of means that lends itself to the expression of the soul in its meditative nakedness. As far as the Master of the Passion of Carlsruhe is concerned, likewise an eclectic, he has more affinity with the school of Alsace than that of Cologne and he probably worked in Swabia as well; if we consider his visionary temperament (*Scenes from the Passion*, Carlsruhe) he should take his place in the center of a triangle the apices of which are the Master of the Legend of St. Ursula, Ratgeb, and Grünewald whose coming he foreshadows in that Alsace over which "handsome Martin" (Schongauer) still reigns.

ALSACE

MARTIN SCHONGAUER

The fact that Albrecht Dürer's chief object on setting off on his tour of Germany was to meet Martin Schongauer at Colmar and that he was greatly upset to hear that the latter had just died, indicates the high esteem in which "handsome Martin" was held in all the German workshops, where they learned a great deal from his engravings if not from his paintings, which were less transportable. After studying with Wolgemut, young Dürer aspired to serve an apprenticeship with a more modern master than the painters of Nuremberg.

To what did Schongauer owe the prestige which he enjoyed far beyond the confines of Alsace? To his technical perfection in the art of engraving as in that of

MARTIN SCHONGAUER – THE HOLY FAMILY. CIRCA 1485 – (0,26; 0,17) KUNSTHISTORISCHES-MUSEUM, VIENNA

HANS FRIES – ST. FRANCIS RECEIVES THE STIGMATA. 1501 – (0,64; 0,35) ALTE PINAKOTHEK, MUNICH

painting, to the suppleness and harmony of his work which was open to every new idea, to a personal talent not too overpowering for his pupils and which helped them to discover their own talent. "Without exaggeration we would be justified in assigning to Schongauer an importance equal to that of Perugino in Italy and Memling in the Low Countries" (Hulftegger). A transmitter of old or new acquisitions, cleverly assimilated and amalgamated in a style that was nevertheless individual, he thus became the master of Grünewald, and was very nearly Dürer's. That, in itself, is no mean achievement.

The proximity of Grünewald tends to make the pilgrims to Colmar do less than justice to Schongauer. The Master of Isenheim remains none the less the great attraction of the Museum of Unterlinden and he dominates everything around him. This in itself is another reason for our attempt to account for Schongauer's fame in his own time and the permanent value of his art to our own. He was born at Colmar and his father was a goldsmith. Prior to 1450 he worked in local studios and died at Brisach in 1491; he is then a typical man of Alsace, in character, origin and education. Caspar Isenmann (circa 1436-1472) whom we assume to be his master could be situated in a subordinate branch on Conrad Witz's genealogical tree; he knew the Basle painters whom he carefully studied, but that was not the basis of his personality; nor was it that experience that he could pass on to young Schongauer. Martin Schön, Hipsch Martin (that is his nickname — "handsome Martin") in all probability met Roger van der Weyden, paid a visit to Flanders and stayed in Cologne. Not unprofitably moreover, and his gain was the greater in that he was careful never merely to imitate those he learned from. Two of Schongauer's major works, different enough from each other to allow us to see the two poles of his personality, the *Adoration of the Shepherds* (Berlin) and the *Madonna of the Rose Garden* (Colmar, 1473), prove how distant he is, aesthetically, from all the great art centers of his time. He is authentic in his sober grandeur, unaffected charm, harmonious, soft, velvety color that has a sweetness that never cloys, a realism that confers nobility on everyday objects and excludes from this familiarity anything that might be banal. Unlike the painters of Cologne he is not a Quietist, nor a tormented soul like the Swabian and Franconian painters. Flesh and spirit both live together in perfect harmony in an art in which equilibrium is the supreme virtue. It is the quality that attracted Dürer and that Grünewald inherited. Both these painters were to go much further than he, of course, but perhaps it was his influence that made this advance possible.

THE MASTERS OF THE CARNATION

The anonymity of the studios, the organization of work in corporations was often the reason why paintings in which it is difficult to distinguish the participation of a strong personality, working among a group of docile disciples, were signed with some kind of emblem. The famous carnation therefore which often served as a signature has been regarded as a studio mark, and critics have assumed that three different collective creations are indicated by this traditional designation of Masters of the Carnation (three are known: emanating from Berne, Freiburg and Zurich) which the Master in each case has not authenticated with his name or monogram but with an object shared in common by all the companions of the *bottega*.

These three Masters of the Carnation present pretty divergent characteristics, inherent in the different media in which they worked, and especially in their different backgrounds, about which we still remain in some uncertainty. Thus, for reasons of stylistic analogy, critics at one time have believed the Zurich Master of the Carnation to be the stained glass painter Peter Reiner who was active in Zurich between 1464 and 1510, or one of his sons, Ludwig or Lienhard; at another, the native of Aargau, Hans Leu the elder who also lived in Zurich between 1488 and 1507. *Herod's Feast* (Berlin, 1490) is a work of pretty impressive classicism, free from the somewhat puerile sentimentality that people liked in that charming artist known as the Master of the Upper Rhine (circa 1420), whose most delightful work is the *Madonna of the Strawberries* of Solothurn, largely Cologne School in inspiration with its candid quietism, ingenuous optimism, akin to Lochner's. It is hard to understand how this innocent and moving painting could have been thrown into the river Aar — if tradition is true — by image-breakers during the period of the religious quarrels.

The works attributed to the Freiburg Master of the Carnation, the Altarpiece of the High Altar of the Cordwainers' church at Freiburg (circa 1479-1480), for example, show such strongly marked composite characteristics that this triptych has been attributed to three painters as different from each other as Albrecht Nent von Rottweil, Paulus von Strasburg and Paulus Löwensprung. Georges Schmidt thinks the painter is a certain Grin Bitlor von Arbon or possibly Heinrich Bichler von Bern. Be that as it may, the Freiburg Master of the Carnation, "trade name" of a workshop owes many of his qualities to Flanders on the one hand, and to Schongauer's Alsace on the other.

The third Master of the Carnation, from Berne, likewise a workshop "trade mark," is less cosmopolitan than the other two. Of the altarpiece of St. John, painted for Berne Cathedral, the panels of which are now scattered, we admire particularly the *St. John in the Wilderness* (Kunsthaus, Zurich) and the *Beheading* (Berne). Less cultivated and refined than the other two, the Berne Master of the Carnation has certain simple, crude almost rustic elements in his work. He has a more natural, not to say naturalistic feeling for landscape and is directly inspired by what he sees. For him trees and rocks are no longer merely pieces of decor; he paints them with an urge to get closer to a perceptible reality, a humble liking for truth, and all the more moving for that.

We come across this feeling for nature, though less gauche and literal, in an artist who is not merely a mediaeval studio master but already a strongly individualized personality, as individuals were to be during the Renaissance — Hans Fries of Freiburg (circa 1460-post 1523). Fries is a realist; he is no longer satisfied with that largely idealized vision of the world enjoyed by the Middle Ages; like Conrad Witz, he is fond of grappling with a frequently recalcitrant reality which he finds it difficult to dominate. He has been regarded as a precursor of the Reformation, and not one of the most timid either; his *Sermon of Saint Anthony* (The Cordwainers' Church, Freiburg, 1505) is essentially modern in its picturesque vehemence and in the passionate individualization of the faces. The two *Visions of St. John* (Zurich, 1505) represent the island of Patmos in the setting and atmosphere of a Swiss lake, faithfully expressed with a very new feeling for landscape. In the scenes of the *Life of the Virgin* which formed part of the Altarpiece of the Virgin Mary (Basle, 1512), he treats recession in a spirit which anticipates that of the Renaissance; in its stylistic conception, still more than by its date, a work of this kind frankly belongs to the sixteenth century during which the second half of the artist's life took place. The usual judgment is that Fries stands half way between flamboyant Gothic and Renaissance; from the first he has retained a certain taste for the decorative, a certain ingenuous, rustic, good-humored note, but this has not prevented him from studying carefully the formal problems of the sixteenth century.

WHILE the preceding century was a period of collective work executed in studios where the different personalities often merged into one characteristic, bearing the stamp of a school, and local traits revealed themselves in Nuremberg, Cologne and Augsburg in a kind of provincial style, affected by many cross currents — for the artists at that time travelled widely and, like artisan "companions", made their tour of Germany before they finally settled down — the sixteenth century saw an increase in the number and influence of contributions from abroad, including Italy, France and the Low Countries. These were frequently connected with the highly instructive "tour" referred to, and at the same time produced a climate favorable for the ripening of strong individualities, with their own ideas, who burst through any notion of "school".

The designations we use in discussing this or that artist in the fifteenth century, his signature, this or that famous painting around which we group a certain number of analogous works, however strongly marked the style and personal aesthetic traits of the particular artist who is merely known as the "Master of...", finally end in a veritable anonymity. In the sixteenth century the number of anonymous works diminishes considerably and is replaced by signed works; the personality of their authors, known through their biography, through their relationship to the intellectual and social life of their time, is separated from the work as such. Whereas the Master of the Life of the Virgin exists to-day only by virtue of the Life of the Virgin, and vanishes into the unknown once we ask questions about his human reality, the great Renaissance artists are known to us and interest us over and above their works. And doubtless it is the spirit of the Renaissance that was responsible for contributing to their lives and artistic creation a whole host of new ideas, original feelings, and above all anxieties, which had hardly troubled their predecessors.

The enlargement of the visual field at that time embraced the natural sciences, discoveries beyond the seas; wonders are watched with curiosity (Dürer made a special journey to observe and draw the two-headed sow of Hanau, he set off at once on hearing about a stranded whale and he made a detailed study of the rhinoceros' peculiarities). But these phenomena were thought of as freaks of nature worthy of scientific analysis, and not as terrifying portents of catastrophes such as frightened the men of the Middle Ages. Progress in mathematics and geometry revealed new spaces from which a new science — perspective — emerged. Every unfamiliar object, treasures from beyond the seas, oriental weapons, shells of fantastic shape, the "sirens" cleverly faked up by Chinese tricksters, found their way into collections. It is the time of the craze for "Wunderkammer" (magic chambers) which were to become so much a feature in the Baroque period.

The passion for the revival of ancient literatures among the humanists, religious anxieties aroused among the first leaders of the Reformation by a new approach to the reading of the Bible and a new conception of human destiny, added a mixture of uneasiness, feverish joy, enthusiasm and melancholy (which is the counterpart, the dark side of enthusiasm), impatience and perplexity to this ardent curiosity which was bound up with every new invention, every form of progress. "What pleasure it is to be alive!" exclaimed Ulrich von Hutten, and Erasmus resented the idea of dying, so eager was he to see everything that was being done in each sphere of knowledge before his eyes, in the fullness of its completion.

The universality of human thought, the constitution of powerful individualities, bent on the solution of every problem, those of the soul, of art, of life in society, the intoxication of learning, of "advancing", of increasing indefinitely one's sum of knowledge and one's potentialities — all this placed man in the center of the universe. A new dignity was conferred on the individual who shook himself free of religious imperatives; proud of his independence, his increasing possibilities, his heavier but honorable responsibilities, the "Renaissance man" was conscious of contributing immense progress to culture and civilization.

It is easy enough to find shadows in this bright picture. Savage ways persisted despite the spread of culture and art (through printing and engraving), and material and moral progress; the Reformation freed man but brought on the atrocities of the Wars of Religion. The War of the Knights and the Peasants' War played havoc with town and countryside and, leaving them in ruins, struck a blow at the consciences of artists, at their faith in man and his qualities; physically, sometimes, since Tilman Riemenschneider is believed to have had his hands cut off — those wonderful woodcarver's hands that he represented on so many occasions... — and Jörg Ratgeb von Gmünd to have been hacked to pieces, in these desperate rebellions.

Violence of this kind called the dignity of man, proclaimed by the humanists, into question again, for the powers of darkness were still as active as and stronger than the powers of light. The chiaroscuro which invaded painting symbolizes this anguish which weighed on the consciences of men who were not prepared merely to rationalize. The supernatural and its materialization in the fantastic, belief in demons, took a new significance from that which it had in the Middle Ages. The instinctive dread of the unknown was increased by the fact that man now felt himself alone in face of all the perils which threatened his reason, his body, his soul, the universe in which he lived. Disturbances that arose from his unconscious and from his relations with the supernatural created a quality of the fantastic in some artists that was more distressing, more metaphysical perhaps than before. The Renaissance man no longer dared play with the Devil and trick him like a simpleton as the man of the old *fabliau* had done. He could only hope that some trickery on the part of the angels would come to his rescue when he was paying the price of his rashly signed pact; for he was alone, confronting the Devil, as he was alone in the face of God.

ALBRECHT DÜRER – FIR-TREES NEAR A POOL OF WATER. WATER COLOR. CIRCA 1495-1497 – (0,262; 0,374)
BRITISH MUSEUM, LONDON

Darkness and light thus shared the physiognomy of that uneasy century, and it is because Albrecht Dürer is the most representative man of that period that his personality and work are made up of these varied and contradictory elements and reflect the shifting aspects of his own genius and of his time as in a faithful mirror.

ALBRECHT DÜRER

Any consideration of the individual artists of this period must begin with a study of Albrecht Dürer, since the characteristics that we have just recognized — being those of the sixteenth century in Germany — find their meeting-place in him, and are resolved in an equilibrium of opposing elements that is remarkably steady and the clear statement of which is rarely clouded[7].

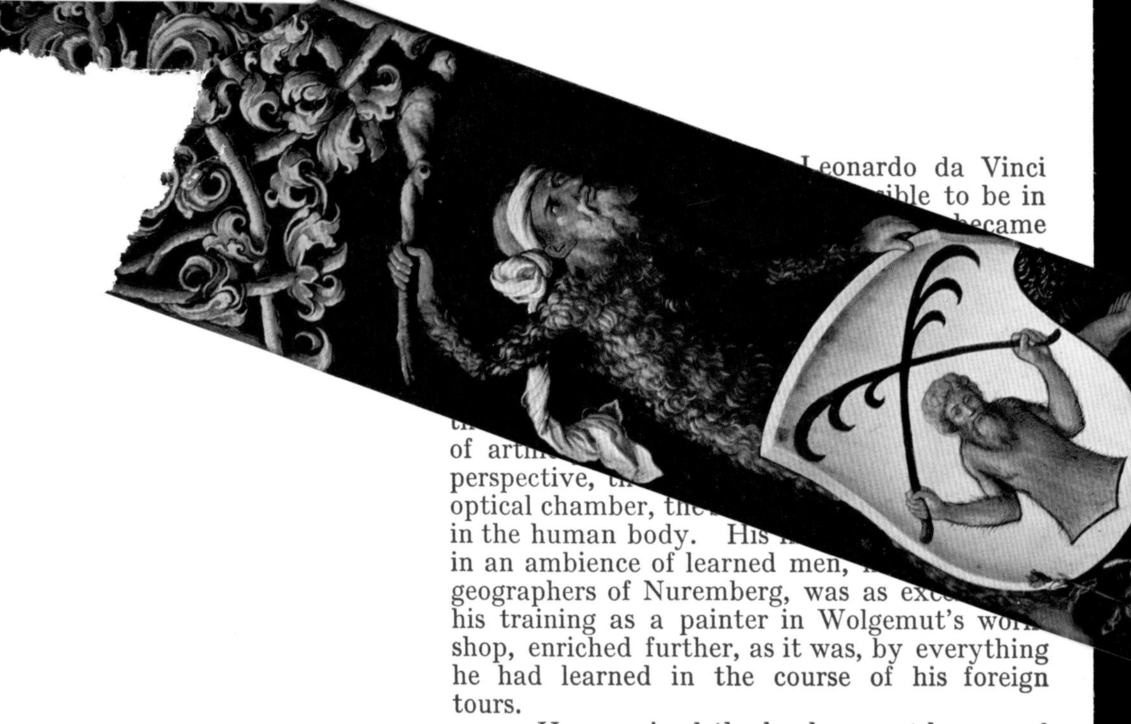

Leonardo da Vinci
...sible to be in
...became

th...
of arth...
perspective, th...
optical chamber, the...
in the human body. His ...
in an ambience of learned men, ...
geographers of Nuremberg, was as exc...
his training as a painter in Wolgemut's wor...
shop, enriched further, as it was, by everything he had learned in the course of his foreign tours.

He examined the landscape at home and abroad with the same loving attention that he had given as a child to a wild flower, an insect on the wing, the fur of a pet rabbit, and he made the discovery that this landscape was worth representing in its own right, not merely as a background to or accessory of a picture. Even when it is a matter of a section of landscape background, like the mountain lake of his *Self-Portrait* of 1498, and the glowing sunset in the *Maries Mourning over the Body of Christ* of Munich (1500), it is possible to separate out such fragments and look at them as pictures for their own sake, each a landscape in its own right and of rare beauty, in the same way as one can look at a background in Bellini, Cima, Carpaccio, all of whom he had studied in Venice. Water colors done direct from nature are no longer — or not necessarily — studies for a future picture; you feel that Dürer has considered the object and its representation worthy of being the subject of a painting, as well as the painting itself.

ALBRECHT DÜRER – COAT-OF-ARMS OF THE KRELL FAMILY – (0,493; 0,159) SHUTTER OF THE OSVOLT KRELL PORTRAIT – ALTE PINAKOTHEK, MUNICH

Even when the landscape is only one element in the composition, it still has to establish and sustain the structure and rhythmic currents in accordance with which the plastic architecture is worked out and organized: *The Adoration of the Trinity by All the Saints* (Vienna, 1511), *The Massacre of the Ten Thousand Martyrs* (Vienna, 1508), *The Feast of the Rosary* (Prague, 1505), *The Adoration of the Magi* of Florence (1504), the *Nativity* of the Paumgärtner Altarpiece (Munich, 1502). The latter composition, with its articulations of massive volumes, thrusts the landscape back into the distance, but also endows it with profound poetry. Love of reality, then, in the landscape, but evocation too, of a musical landscape, symphonically conceived or melodically unfolded, that is to say, transcending reality; transcending reality also in his depiction of the human frame which was of such absorbing interest to him. To him it was the great secret, or part of the "great secret" about which he questioned Jacopo de Barbari in Nuremberg and the Italian painters he met in Venice. The *Adam and Eve* of Madrid (1507), the *Lucretia* of Munich (1518) were studies from life — and he himself often posed as his own model — worked on later in accordance with the principles of a theoretical formula, based on ideal beauty and super-accidental truth.

From the Humanists, his friends, he had learned the theories of the Ancients on these questions, read books contained in the libraries of the scholars who encouraged him and subsidized his journeys. The laws of numbers, precepts of "divine proportion", notions of the Ancients on "humors," their knowledge of the stars and natural forces, were a constant source of inspiration, and the major work of his maturity almost on the eve of his death, the *Four Apostles* of Munich (1526) is certainly as well as an act of homage to the Reformation and its precursors whose friendship he enjoyed,

ALBRECHT DÜRER – COAT-OF-ARMS OF THE KRELL FAMILY – (0,493; 0,159) SHUTTER OF THE OSVOLT KRELL PORTRAIT – ALTE PINAKOTHEK, MUNICH

ALBRECHT DÜRER – OSVOLT KRELL – (0,48; 0,38) ALTE PINAKOTHEK, MUNICH

Luther and Melanchthon, and whose ideas he had followed since 1518, the representation of the Four Humors, embodied in these figures of the Church Fathers whose characters he had so subtly analyzed.

For these strong personalities of the Renaissance, the individual is everything; the artist never tired of studying the infinite number of traits, physical, moral, psychological which distinguish one man from his fellows and make him a unique, strongly individualized being. The success of the portrait at this time, above all, the self-portrait, provides evidence of this shifting of interest from the collective to the personal. Dürer with Rembrandt is the painter who studied his own personality with the most perspicacious attention. For Albrecht Dürer a true portrait must be *faithful;* which means it must embrace the whole personality, not only the exterior appearance but also the often veiled complexity of the inner soul. It is not even a mere psychological and formal curiosity which leads him, as it did Holbein, to examine the mystery of the consciences that open up before him; he is eager to enter into complete possession of this mixture of flesh and spirit that sits before him; to the visible being present before him he adds the infinite sum of invisible and potential qualities.

It is by virtue of this truly magic operation that Dürer's portraits acquired an almost unique intensity; it is manifest in the direct modelling of the faces which are moved by tyrannical passions, likewise in the magnetic authority of the glances which fix the spectators' eye as if they were seizing hold of him and did not intend to let him go. In exchange for this procedure by which the painter has emptied the model of all his mysteries in order to pass them into the portrait, the latter in its turn forces the onlooker to capitulate and surrender himself completely. The *Osvolt Krell* of Munich (1499), the *Bernard van Orley* of Dresden (1521), the *Jacob Muffel* and *Jerome Holzschuher* of Berlin, by the absolute truth of the faces and charge of interior life that emanates from the look, exercise an irresistible fascination over whoever stops to contemplate them.

In everything capable of simple, formal treatment, like his Virgins, often inspired directly by the Venetians, some of whom are charming (the *Virgin with the Goldfinch*, Berlin, 1506; the *Virgin and Child*, Vienna, 1512), Raphaelesque idealism is allied to a healthy, Germanic robustness, and then, piety, less intense, is replaced by an exuberant sensuality; this is not the true Dürer, nor do we see him in his ambitious religious compositions in which he is not noticeably the superior of his Franconian masters.

In his handling of the real landscape, bathed in music and poetry to such an extent that we are tempted to discover a direct link between him and Friedrich's romantic landscape, in the imperious and almost savage violence of the "Faustian" portraits – which implied the visible and invisible world, the present and the future, he represents the constant of German genius in its strangest and most powerful manifestation [8].

Engraving still more than painting lent itself to that attitude towards the supernatural which occupies so large a place in Dürer's work; the *Four Witches*, the *Doctor's Dream, The Rape of Amymone, the Knight, Death and the Devil,* the famous and inexhaustible *Melancolia,* to quote only a few examples, seem like soundings made by a fretful imagination and visionary temperament in the limitless realm of the unknown and the supernatural. The *Apocalypse,* above all, brings off that *tour de force,* so rarely successful, of harmoniously blending the seen and the visionary, objective reality and the almost unrepresentable fantasy of the Revelation.

So powerful and dominating a genius was unlikely to create a "school", the less so, in that Dürer's taste for solitude, in which he differed from Cranach and many of his contemporaries, stopped him from surrounding himself with numerous pupils. A large number of German painters bear the stamp of his energetic influence but the only ones we can pick out from those who were really pupils, in the precise sense of the term, that is who worked under his direction, are a Wolf Traut (circa 1486-1520) whose personality seems somewhat submerged in his zeal for imitating the master and Hans Süss von Kulmbach (circa 1480-1522) who was equally sensitive to the lessons of Jacopo de Barbari and the seductions of the Venetians.

MATTHIAS GRÜNEWALD

Doubtless the Master of Colmar whom we always know as Matthias Grünewald, the man whom Melanchthon — who considered him the equal of Dürer — knew as "Mathis", may be a Mathis Gothardt-Neihardt who died in 1528. In our present uncertainty, it is perhaps better to follow the tradition and refer to him simply as Grünewald, whatever his real name may have been[9].

The forceful originality of his genius, the visionary intensity of a highly spiritualized, yet realist art, together with a certain lingering archaism in this contemporary of the "modern German man" that Dürer was, went to the formation of a fascinating and amazing personality. Nikolaus Pevsner has said of him that he was "the last great artist of the Middle Ages", and it would certainly appear that his sensibility, his conception of the world belonged less to the Renaissance than to the Gothic period. Although he was a court-painter[10], the problems which absorbed him are not those which interested his contemporaries.

This strange man whom Sandrart, more strangely still, called the "German Correggio," had collaborated with Dürer in the Heller Altarpiece, but his idiom seems to be at the opposite pole from the Master of Nuremberg's, to such an extent that the proximity of these very divergent geniuses was to give the Heller Altarpiece a somewhat heterogeneous appearance.

It is easy enough to emphasize and elaborate a facile comparison between the man of the Middle Ages and the man of the Renaissance, but the truth is that Grünewald belongs to the German tradition as much as Dürer, and was probably even more bound up with later developments. The *Isenheim Altarpiece* in fact foreshadows the Baroque, Romanticism and Expressionism, and it is in this light that we compare Grünewald to present-day painters, even the Surrealists, and consider

MATTHIAS GRÜNEWALD – ISENHEIM ALTARPIECE. CIRCA 1515 – (2,69; 3,07)
CENTRAL PANEL OF THE CRUCIFIXION. COLMAR MUSEUM

it justifiable to acknowledge the vast potentiality and future that lay inherent in this Altarpiece. But it is over Grünewald's works that we must linger, for it is in them that the real personality of the artist appears in all its grandiose and fascinating strangeness. The relationship between the spirituality which inspired the Stuppach *Madonna*, the *Little Crucifixion* of Basle and that in Karlsruhe, the *Meeting of St. Maurice and St. Erasmus* of Munich and the vicissitudes which religious thought underwent at the period when these works were painted, are subsidiary concerns. Grünewald is, beyond all doubt, closer to the German mystics of the Middle Ages than to the men of the Reformation. He depicts the devils in the *Temptation of St. Anthony* as one who himself had some difficulty in escaping the Devil's clutches.

Grünewald lived in continual intimacy with the supernatural, to such a point that to him, as to El Greco or Bosch, the supernatural came as second nature. The way he transmutes the traditional symbols of theology into various shapes is proof enough of the violence with which his visions seized him and opened the flood gates of his imagination. Every aspect of visionary art is revealed in the Isenheim Altarpiece (Colmar, painted in all probability between 1512 and 1515), each wing of this great mystical treatise in pictorial form shows a well-defined supernatural state, — the dazzling image of the Angel in the *Annunciation*, Christ's face dissolving into light in the *Resurrection*, the *Angel Concert*... What does it matter if we recognize facial resemblances between the demons of the *Temptation* and the monsters of Schongauer whose pupil he is thought to have been?

The painter of the Isenheim Antonites endowed his female figures with an idealized grace, a spiritual beauty which few of his contemporaries achieved, even outside Germany, and which the Romantics looked at and appreciated when they restored religious painting to a place of honor. The Madonna's face is spiritualized to the point almost of divinity, and round her and the Child the concord and harmony of the elements unfold with a powerful and calm grandeur, reminiscent of the cosmic significance of the Magna Mater of the Ancients. All about her radiates like a sublime aureole the dazzling powdering of gold and fire like a flaming sunset. When ordinary objects intervene in the episodes of the Holy Scriptures, they are clothed in the humble nobility of their usefulness. Such objects take their place in the *Isenheim Altarpiece* with the quiet dignity of old servants. If Grünewald painted a face transfigured by esctasy or grief and a bundle of wood or an earthenware bowl with the same love, the reason is that as far as he was concerned the whole of reality is subordinate to the supernatural world.

Side by side with fantastic details — statues that stand away from the architecture, gesticulate in impassioned discussions, the fabulous butterflies of the *Angel Concert*, the vast shining cliffs which mark off the frontiers of the visible world in the panel of the *Temptation* — the familiar thing is also present, implied in the incredible incident, proving that this fantastic element is never merely gratuitous.

Everything is vision in Grünewald, and everything is true : true in the world of material things and in the world of the soul which he does not separate off. "You go to Colmar to look for Schongauer and you discover Grünewald," said Böcklin. It is the Altar of the Spirit in the West," said Martin Buber, and "Colmar is as important as Benares." It is possible that the spiritual organization of the Isenheim Altarpiece, built up on the theme of suffering and salvation, was suggested to the artist

LUCAS CRANACH – CRUCIFIXION. 1503 – (1,38; 0,99) ALTE PINAKOTHEK, MUNICH

by the Abbot of the Antonites, Guido Guersi, who commissioned the work and who probably figured in it as the Saint Anthony of the *Encounter in the Wilderness*, in which Grünewald was perhaps Saint Paul. Grünewald is really more likely to have been Saint Sebastian, but we do not know the painter's age when he painted the Altarpiece in question; certain scholars assign it to the year 1461 or 1462, others to the years 1475 to 1480, a whole generation later. Of all the folding altarpieces this is the richest in symbolism, theological concepts, sacred allegories; and the progressive "opening" of the shutters revealed a complete doctrine of the Redemption to the congregation.

The view reserved for ordinary days was that showing the *Crucifixion*, flanked by two fixed shutters representing St. Anthony and St. Sebastian. On fête days the first pair of shutters was opened up which depicted episodes from the life of Christ, the *Annunciation*, the *Maternity*, the *Resurrection*. If the first view with its pictures of the *Crucifixion* — and what a pitiable victim we see, devoured by wounds, pitiful and repulsive in the darkness that covers the earth — evokes suffering, death and, at the same time, salvation, the open shutters relate the wonderful story of the Savior and his Mother in its everyday reality, surrounded by fantastic elements like a strange girdle. The third arrangement of the Altarpiece, devoted to the feast of St. Anthony, glorified the monastery and the founder of the Order: its central panel, gleaming with gold and colors, told of the eminent earthly virtues of St. Anthony, his austerities, his victories over the devil and his heavenly glory. In this way the altarpiece in the various adaptations prescribed by the liturgy, corresponded to a true theological account. But it is unfolded in the very atmosphere of the miraculous, the illumination of the supernatural and transcendental which the turmoil of ideas spread by the Renaissance and humanism had failed to rid of the powerful suggestion they continued to exercise upon men's imaginations.

We are justified in supposing that Grünewald's impressive use of the fantastic struck and affected his contemporaries, but certain gaps in his biography prevent us from knowing who his pupils — if, indeed, he had any — were[11]. But his influence on Hans Baldung is at all events indisputable.

LUCAS CRANACH

Lucas Cranach (1472-1553) is often picked out as the most "German" of the masters of the German Renaissance, for his nervous and vibrating line, his cold, brilliant, enamel-like color, the medievalism of his method of narration, whether it concerns episodes from ancient history, the scriptures or mythology, and his remoteness from the plastic problems that preoccupied Italy. It was a country that he knew only at second-hand — since, unlike Dürer, he had never travelled there — from drawings, engravings and the Italian elements in the painters of the Low Countries, Matsys and Gossaert in particular whom he studied assiduously. His art still retains a popular aspect and even his imagination belongs to the last phase of Gothic, and embodies its most subtle charms.

LUCAS CRANACH
1532 – (0,37;
STÄDELSCHESKUNS
FRANKFURT-AM

LUCAS CRANACH – THE ELECTOR OF SAXONY. 1532 – (0,675; 0,

The influences in which his early works are steepe
f the "Danube School" from which he borrowed his
ealism is so perfectly adapted to the dramatic scenes of
or which the Middle Ages, spilling over its chronological
ion. His association with scholars and men of letters,
he very early years of the century, he was in contact with
uspinian whose portraits he painted, then at Wittenberg wh
elationship with the great scholars of the Reformation that
s "our dear cousin," opened up vast domains of legend and
hilosophic thought and theology to this painter whose activity
d of his life — witness his self-portrait done at the age of s
ho probably had little time for extensive reading.

There was however nothing literary about Cranach's work. He was a Court painter in the services of the princes of Saxony, assiduously engaged in recording their portraits, festivities and sports, decorating their castles, and so devoted to his masters that he accompanied them in their captivity and shared their imprisonment. His output was phenomenal, and if the workshop he directed can claim a good share in works attributed to him, his hand is clearly recognizable in the paintings which have been authenticated; his two sons, Hans who died at Bologna in 1537 and was considered by his contemporaries as the most remarkable of his pupils, and Lucas Cranach "the Younger," who inherited the workshop after his father's death and made little attempt to break away from the imitation of a style which had proved successful, were content to follow in their father's tracks.

This workshop method is a relic of medievalism in Cranach; likewise the fertility of his popular, almost rustic imagination, fascinated as he was by the marvellous, yet passionately interested in nature and at the same time ready to respond to every prompting of his imagination. This quality figures for example in his representation of Hermes and the Trojan Prince in the legend of the *Judgment of Paris*, where we see the splendid and complicated armor, engraved and plumed, of the knights of Saxony who were his contemporaries. The period when he was temporarily infatuated with the classical ideal of beauty as manifested by Leonardo or Giorgione, the fruit of his friendship with Jacopo de Barbari, was only a brief interlude.

Cranach's paintings thus possess a powerful and attractive originality, and a musicality which distinguish them from those of any other artist. His portraits may aim less at being "portraits of the soul" than Dürer's or Holbein's, and sometimes the portraits of the princes look like sumptuous versions of popular prints heightened with gold and rare colors; his Electors of Saxony and their wives are on occasion transformed into fabulous creatures beneath their excessive ornaments and jewelry; nevertheless Cranach remains the faithful, and at times, ironic interpreter of the fashions of his time and their dazzling luxury, composing unreal figures, comparable to the statuettes of Swabian or Franconian goldsmiths. He is intrigued by detail; but he goes a step beyond, so that everything melts into a unity that is possessed of a lively and joyful symphonic sonority.

One of the problems he frequently tackled all through his career was that of the representation of the nude; a problem in which the individuality of the artist generally coincides with the taste of his time. It would be interesting to know whether fashions in clothes and their influence on women's lives did in fact transform the female body between 1508 (the engraving of the *Judgment of Paris*) and 1530 (*Apollo and Diana*, of Berlin, for example). In the engraving, the three goddesses are hefty wenches with short legs and attractive in a heavy way. The Coburg *Lucretia* (circa 1518) was refined down through the artist's association with the Italians whose canons of beauty had been expounded to him by Jacopo de Barbari whom he had met at Wittenberg.

It was by taking the idealized Flemish-Italian nude as a starting-point that Cranach worked out, particularly in the *Eve* (1528, Florence) and onwards, those feminine figures who are the very signature of his imagination and his genius as a painter. Just as his Saxon princes in court dress often finish under Cranach's brush by resembling giant coleopters with glistening wings, his female nudes have the paradoxical, piquant and provoking charm of an insect-woman, caught in the act of her metamorphosis. They increase their seductiveness by making use of perverse accessories: a vast velvet hat with plumes and ribbons, like an immense corolla surmounting a thin and pale stalk, a transparent veil daintily spread over objects it fails to mask, thus arousing curiosity and desire all the more. If we compare the *Judgment of Paris* of 1529 (Metropolitan Museum) with the old engraving, we are still confronted with a Paris dressed as the hero of a chivalrous romance, but the three women have acquired the prettiness of an almost ugly ambiguity with their exaggerated elongation, which intrigues the mind rather than the senses and flatters the somewhat fantastic and sophisticated unreality of an Aulic civilization which inherited from Gothic flamboyant, and is preparing to introduce into Baroque that love for sinuous, whirling forms associated with *Schnorkel* decoration of strapwork and twisted metal threads.

Had the full-scale decorations that Lucas Cranach carried out for the castles of the Electors of Saxony survived, we should have a more precise knowledge of this artist who is incompletely represented even by his great altarpieces. Among the eulogistic descriptions applied to him by his contemporaries occurs this: "*Pictor celerrimus*", engraved on his tomb. The speed for which he was praised is eminently that of the decorator accustomed to brushing in huge palace compositions. It is now impossible to determine to what extent his small-format drawings or pictures can be regarded as studies for large compositions. The representation of the *Stag-Hunt* done for Elector Frederick the Wise (Vienna, 1529), gives us an idea of what the great decorative compositions, conceived somewhat in the manner of French and Flemish tapestries, looked like. This depiction of a hunt with the fidelity of the animal-painter's truth to life, the accuracy of its landscape, still in the Danube School tradition, was to be the beginning of a *genre* destined to be extremely fertile; it is furthermore important for our knowledge of a Cranach who is not so well known as the painter of nudes and portraits, a Cranach whose dynamic energy was causing the fabric founded on the traditions of the last phase of Gothic to crack on every side.

ALBRECHT ALTDORFER AND THE DANUBE SCHOOL

If Reichlich really did exert an influence on the painter who, along with Caspar David Friedrich, deserves to be called the "master of German landscape," it cannot be recognized in what goes to make Albrecht Altdorfer's greatness and his contribution of genius to German art of the sixteenth century, namely, a conception of nature in which, as with the Romantics, the seen is the garment of the unseen. An affinity has been noted more than once, particularly by Benesch, between the mystical nature cult of Paracelsus and the panic-stricken forests of Altdorfer in which primitive powers lurk amidst the dense foliage, and legendary monsters drag their heavy bodies among huge pine trees with their cloaks of moss and lichen.

For Altdorfer nature ceases to be a mere pretext for experiment, a realistic basis of observation and representation. It might be said to be spiritualized in the sense that it is peopled with forces in which the spirit of the Earth breathes — the so-called Erdgeist of the Urfaust — and mingles the affairs of the soul with man's elemental instincts. Altdorfer's most characteristic landscapes, those of *St. George* (Munich, 1510), the *Family of the Wild Man* (Berlin, 1507), the *Martyrdom of St. Catherine* (Vienna, 1506 or 1507) are those which show a violent animism; nature identifies itself with the drama of which it is the scene, it exhales anger, hatred, cruelty, danger; it is at once the reflection and the echo of the passions which trouble men's hearts. Anticipating the Romantics such as Oehme, Carus, Blechen by several centuries, Altdorfer endowed the elements of the landscape with a solemn, savage, wild majesty which corresponded to the character of the torturers, woodland demi-gods, dragon-slaying knights.

This conception of the landscape which figures as a whole entity, charged with emotion and furious passion, starting with his first paintings and the works of his twenty-fifth and his thirtieth year, was not to undergo much subsequent change; it developed, however, in the composition of opulent, musical color which was more concerned with discovering the key of cosmic communion than with symbolism, and which found its climax in the supernatural sunset of the *Battle of Arbela* painted in 1529 to adorn the new castle of the Duke of Bavaria, Wilhelm IV, an enterprise in which Bartel Beham, Jorg Breu and his brother Burgkmair also collaborated and where Altdorfer left the masterpiece of his maturity (Munich).

The calmer, realistic landscapes, several of which recall the backgrounds of certain Venetian painters whom he appears not to have known, at least not at that time, of the Altar of St. Florian executed in 1518 for the Abbot Peter Maurer (Germanisches Nationalmuseum, Nuremberg), are expressions of another aspect of the complex and still enigmatic personality of an artist whose genius appears, to whoever analyses it, more and more fascinating and disconcerting. He thought of the landscape as something worth considering in its own right and for its own sake, sharing in this the opinion of the water colorist Dürer, his contemporary, who, at roughly the same date as Altdorfer was painting a *View of the Danube Valley* (Munich), was executing on the spot a series of Tyrolese and Franconian landscapes that are a strange and fascinating novelty at a time when nature was subordinated to the figure and relegated to the role of background and setting.

Altdorfer's aim of establishing perfect homogeneity between the human figure and the space in which the waves of his anxieties and passions are prolonged, his belief in an emotional relationship between man and the world around him, his achievement of this harmony, this pantheistic fusion through the use of form and color, treating the latter as a kind of primitive force which infuses its own particular quality of vitality to the object painted, all these things combine to endow his work with a supernatural beauty and an individual importance in the history of German art and, indeed, the history of art in general.

Never, in point of fact, had any artist, before or after, attempted this paradoxical and perilous enterprise of representing one of the greatest battles in history in a picture of such modest dimensions. He depicted in it moreover the participation of the elements in the conflict, where, like Homer's gods presiding over the exploits of Greek and Trojan heroes, they bear witness to Alexander the Great's victory. They themselves become colossal forces, pitted against each other — matter and light, air and mountains, engaged in a titanic struggle which reduces to insignificance — as the artist no doubt intended — the human appetites, ambitions and greed, responsible for this clash between the armies of Alexander and those of Darius.

In this composition, amazing in boldness of conception as in sureness of execution and in which the tiniest detail of a piece of armor, a plume, lance or harness, is treated with the scrupulous care of the miniaturist, expert in all matters to do with military science, Altdorfer aimed at making a Paracelsian contrast between the microcosm of human passions and the actions they engender and the vast outside expanse, with its suggestion of an infinity of worlds, and above all this, the "eye of light" in the storm center of a whirling maelstrom, ready to hide behind its eyelids of cloud and shadow.

In the *Two St. Johns* of the Katharinenspital of Regensburg-Stadtamhof (1511), you can already perceive the landscape elements of the *Battle of Arbela*, but they are treated in the minor key of one of those intimate, hermit scenes which were so much in favor among German painters of the sixteenth century. The remarkable thing here in an eminently static action in which allusion can be made only to an imaginary conversation, since the Apostle and the Evangelist never met, is the pride of place accorded to nature and — in the absence of any reference to war — the composition of a landscape of a kind that anticipates the *Battle of Arbela*, with the aura of light in this case at the spot where the Virgin Mary appears, and the development in recession of his mountain and sea distances... The elemental life of the water, plants, rocks, trees participates, so to speak, in this "holy conversation" to use the Italian expression, and brings along with it the consecration of the primordial earth forces. The place occupied by plant life in the conception which Altdorfer had of a universe in which nothing was inanimate, may be compared to the importance which Philipp Otto Runge attributed to the flower in the nineteenth century, in accordance with the laws of "correspondence" which have their origin more in a nature mystique than in symbolism.

We know from contemporary documents which supplement — if not very completely — the works themselves, of which nothing remains, that Altdorfer in the last years of his life was actively concerned with architecture, having become an official of great importance in his native town of Regensburg where he was probably born, circa 1480, and where, according to the texts we possess, he acquired the freedom of the city in 1505 and became its mayor and died in February, 1538. The *Susanna and the Elders* of Munich (1526) probably marks the beginning, not necessarily of his activity as a builder, but of his dreams of architecture on a monumental scale. The famous Biblical episode is here reduced to an insignificant part of the picture, almost entirely occupied by a vast building, several stories high, whereas the bathing scene itself which is extremely chaste — the lady is merely having her feet

ALBRECHT ALTDORFER – THE BATTLE OF ARBELA. 1529 – (1,58; 1,20) DETAIL. ALTE PINAKOTHEK, MUNICH

washed and her long hair combed — takes place at the edge of a forest whose trees border on the terraces. What lingers in our minds above all, and even more than Altdorfer's architectural ideas, intriguing though they are, in contrast with the crowd which inhabits this enormous palace and its polychromatic, arcade-intersected mass, is the tranquillity of the wood with its light shadows and delicate flowers; some of these which look like hollyhocks recur so often in Altdorfer that we are justified in assuming that it was not so much a personal predilection for these flowers as a magic or allegorical significance which he attributed to them.

Well before the time of Elsheimer and Rembrandt, Altdorfer, as a corollary to his cosmic feeling for a landscape that was both real and fantastic, surreal in its fantastic reality, studied the supremely spiritual function of light. More and more this "color" conceived by him as of the same nature as the elements, is saturated with light; not to such a point that its form dissolves completely and becomes dematerialized into pure spirituality as in the *Resurrection* in the Isenheim Altarpiece, but on the contrary, enough in order to take its due and proper place in the composition.

This discovery of the dramatic landscape which ultimately exists in its own right results from the very nature of the setting which the German artists had before their eyes and which, naturally enough, provided the setting of their pictures. We breathe in them the air of the Thuringian forest, the Black Forest, Franconia or Saxon Switzerland, and what began by being *respiration* becomes *inspiration.* This setting did indeed possess a power of stimulus, a tragic intensity which transforms the pine forests of Hans Baldung, Matthias Grünewald or Altdorfer into a primitive, primeval forest, an *Urwald,* a virgin forest in the literal sense, in which man feels truly himself and into which he may not venture with impunity.

In the same way as sixteenth century France reflects the gentle undulations of the Loire valley in its paintings and the Venetian painters exploit the iridescence of the lagoon waters and the grotesquely strange silhouettes of the Dolomites, German painting finds its ideal setting in forest. This unity of character is to be met in the schools of the Renaissance, in a native of Alsace like Baldung, a Swiss like Graf, and in the Swabian Altdorfer.

HANS BALDUNG GRIEN

Eclectic as he is in his technical education, since he made his début in the Schongauer tradition — which for a long time predominated in Strasburg — and entered Dürer's workshop before his twentieth year and was probably greatly impressed by Grünewald's genius, Hans Baldung also shows that kinship with the forest which gives so profound and vigorous an accent to the *Deposition* (Berlin, 1515) and to the *Rest During the Flight from Egypt* (Nuremberg, 1513). His remarkable engravings of horses prove that he was conscious of the mysterious, almost supernatural and magic nature of an animal which Germanic traditions felt to be a creature apart, almost sacrosanct.

Although Baldung was responsive to this ancient background of impressions, rather than beliefs — to which the name superstitions is sometimes given — he was an educated man, open to new ideas and the intellectual currents of his time. When he painted the Altarpiece of the High Altar of Freiburg cathedral in Breisgau (1516), it was as a scholar, fully aware of what the theological program of such a composition demanded, but also as one who had never lost touch with the element of magic that the popular mind clings to instinctively. He discovered this element of wonder in the strange and dramatic effects of light, in the singular harmonies he obtained in contrasts between the pallor of naked figures, often cold and leaden-hued, and the

HANS BALDUNG – ADORATION OF THE MAGI. 1507 – (1,21; 0,70) NATIONALGALERIE, BERLIN-DAHLEM

deadened, almost extinct warmth of the green or black backgrounds with their yawning depths of darkness.

He had become familiarized with the mythological fables and allegories from the writings and conversations of his Humanist friends as well as from his study of Italian engravings, but he brings to his treatment of both an authentic power, a realism free of any literary element, a deep understanding of the intimate significance of the picture. The presence of the cat squatting at the feet of the figure representing Music has been considered enigmatic, but it is justified perhaps by some popular saying or scholarly allusion. What is more significant is the violent division of the landscape into two areas, one very light, the other intensely dark, the forest becoming almost a grotto and the grotto vibrating like a sound box, in response to the lute strings which the beautiful young woman is plucking.

One of the themes in which Baldung's strange imagination delights, in strict harmony with the spirit of his time and conscious of a kind of sinister hedonism, charged with desperate voluptuousness, is that of Death seizing hold of the Quick. The dramatic narration of the *Danse Macabre* which conjures up all ranks and conditions of men, all stages of human life, one after the other, is summed up in the most arresting episode, *Death and the Maiden*, and the episode, too, in his "morality" (Basle, 1517). The gesture has a horrible and terrifying truth; the voluptuous flesh turns weak and faint under the embrace of skeleton hands so cruelly laid on this supple and desirable body which might well have been borrowed from the Venetian painters.

Baldung therefore appears as one or the most representative artists of a period when a certain element of medieval ingenuousness still lingered on even amidst the flood of new ideas, eager to sweep away Gothic archaism and outmoded habits of thought. He has a foot in both periods; this is particularly so in the *Miracle of St. Dorothea* (Prague, 1516) in which the winter landscape with its snow-laden sky, bare trees, hillsides shrivelled in the frost, is of a wholly modern sensibility. Yet in the same picture the medieval double episode occurs and furthermore, the mysterious child who offers flowers and fruits to the Saint's executioner, Child Christ though he is, looks like a little Dionysus with his sturdy limbs and round head, garlanded with flowers.

NIKLAS MANUEL DEUTSCH

The originality of the Bernese lansquenet painter, Niklas Manuel Deutsch, lies essentially in the interpretation he gives to the episodes of the myth which his fantasy prompts him to treat and the technique he employs so that the rapidity of the actual physical execution should follow the whims of his imagination at the same speed and with the same freedom. Thus he invents at one and the same moment new elements of a story which can be perpetually renewed, and the pictorial matter which he employs, the thin distemper, extremely transparent and a fluid, calligraphic line, exploiting the canvas itself — both means of plastic expression adapted to the narrative style. This is the idiom Manuel Deutsch exploited in his *Judgment of Paris* (Basle, 1520) or *Pyramus and Thisbe* (Basle, 1529). Twice — 1516 and 1520 — he went on military campaigns to Lombardy as a member of Swiss companies of lansquenets raised for the king of France. It does not seem likely that he actually participated in any battles since he was enrolled as a secretary, but it is evident that this life of adventure and wandering satisfied his restless and violent temperament. Later, he embraced the anti-papistry of the Reformed religion with a fiery sectarian-

NIKLAS MANUEL DEUTSCH – THE JUDGMENT OF PARIS. CIRCA 1524 – (2,18; 1,58) KUNSTMUSEUM, BASLE

ism, serving this cause with his pen in the carnival farces spiced with irreverent buffoonery and theological arguments with the same carefree pugnacity which had sent him to Italy at the age of thirty.

These stays in Italy which did not outlast the period of time fixed by custom for mercenaries on these short-term enlistments had little effect on his art. Immune to aesthetic influences, the work which went on in his interior world is related to his personal reflections on life, what one might call his private philosophy. His concept of form, his professional recipes are fundamentally his own; he owes nothing to Italy — he brought back at most a dramatic, pessimistic philosophy, dominated by the feeling of the presence of the devil and the perpetual evidence of death which threatens the warrior and, indeed, every man each minute of the day. This preoccupation with death is the inspiration behind the majority of his religious works, the last of which, the *Altarpiece of St. Anthony* has the date 1520, the time when Deutsch was becoming an uncompromising anti-papist; the canvases prior to that date are all profane, and in the two panels of the *Temptation of St. Anthony* which are in the Berne Museum, the temptation by demons and the one in which the Devil appears himself in the form of a young woman, it will be noticed that the emphasis is on the picturesque, realist details — one of the demons brandishes the customary weapon of mercenary soldiers, the mace, that has the shape of a flail, the *Morgenstern;* beneath the sumptuous dress of the Devil in female guise advances a huge bird's leg lengthened with long claws — and on the landscape, which was probably where the painter's chief interest lay.

We inevitably compare Manuel's chiaroscuro painting on the same subject (Basle, circa 1517) with Baldung's *Death and the Maiden;* should we look on it as a study for one of the panels of the *Danse Macabre* which he had been commissioned to do by the Dominicans of Berne to decorate their graveyard in an edifying manner? We are tempted to think so, although our knowledge of these sinister scenes with their hideous vitality is restricted to contemporary copies. Baldung represented the obscene embrace in a somber and stormy forest setting; in Manuel's painting a horrible gleefulness directs the skeleton's hand which lifts the girl's dress and claws the very spot where she had sinned and most enjoyed her sinful act. She is not naked in the mythological convention, but clothed in an elegant and careless splendor like a soldier's tart, the kind who followed companies of lansquenets in the hope of booty from the Italian wars; and the Renaissance columns, heavily decorated, the altar surmounted with a chilly goddess, unwarmed by the censer that burns before her, add an ironic magnificence to the frightful caress of the mustached skeleton that is dressed in torn shreds of decaying flesh.

It is in paintings such as these that we must look for the real Manuel Deutsch, the puny man with the convulsive face (Berne, 1530), turned Protestant polemist, the visionary dreamer, haunted by the ghosts of old battlefields, rather than in the sage artist, a prisoner of tradition who, in 1515, painted the *Altarpiece of St. Anne* (Berne) to the order of the confraternity of painters (St. Luke) and the goldsmiths (St. Eloi). A minute realism which describes in detail all the tools in the artisan's workshop appears like a medieval, naive and archaic tradition in which the artist still lingers in his thirtieth year; but the true reality is what the visible and invisible together compose and is made simultaneously evident in the artist's grasp of whatever is perceptible, his intuitive consciousness of the supernatural and uncanny familiarity with the miraculous.

THE LANSQUENET PAINTERS:
URS GRAF, HANS LEU THE YOUNGER

As opposed to Manuel who probably never wielded a sword and a mace on the battlefields of Lombardy and who ended up inside the skin of an important Berne citizen, Urs Graf and Hans Leu the Younger did not consider war as a secondary, lucrative profession but as the *métier* of their free choice; by character and temperament they were soldiers first and foremost; painters only later on. Thus their works which are of a singular beauty are relatively rare in comparison with Manuel's and have the atmosphere and stamp of the perilous life led by those independent, unsociable, quarrelsome, yet open handed individuals who were imprisoned on not a few occasions — Leu at Wellenberg, Graf in the Spalentor at Basle. Leu died in the same battle in which Zwingli perished, as befitted a lansquenet who had fought with such heroism at Marignano.

The habit and probably also the necessity of dividing their time between profitable war expeditions and the studio lends the work of these painters — as it did in the case of Manuel — a very special dramatic quality which puts as unmistakable a seal on their painting as the dagger which they, like him, append to their initials. Urs Graf and Hans Leu both underwent an excellent training as craftsmen, the former with his father who was a Basle goldsmith; he began by learning the paternal profession which he practised for some time, just as Manuel had been a stained glass window artist — more than a hint of which we see in his coloring. As for the father of Hans Leu the Younger who was also his master, it is thought nowadays that he was that anonymous artist called the Zurich Master of the Carnation; his son continued for some time the habit of adding a red carnation to his monogram. He worked with Dürer at Nuremberg, but it was more especially with Baldung, who took him on as a pupil at Freiburg in Breisgau, that he learned to develop and refine the violent idiom which was his characteristic.

Hans Leu was born in Zurich about 1490; he was killed at the battle of Kappel in 1531 in which Manuel also took part; the files of lawsuits against him contain the sum total of our knowledge of his irregular life, his quarrels with his wife and the Zurich authorities. Aesthetically he is very close to Baldung, with whom he had close affinities — his tragic feeling for life, his awareness of the presence of death and a familiarity with the fantastic. Technically he adopted, like Manuel, the method of painting with distemper on canvas.

The personality of Urs Graf is more complex and his artistic training more varied. A goldmith by profession, he was also an engraver on coins and a stained glass window artist. An extraordinary colorist in his drawings, he made use of colored papers on which the pen or chalk described capricious arabesques, each movement of his hand corresponding to a macabre and ironic invention that evokes François Villon and his *Ballade des Pendus*. His favorite subjects are borrowed from military life; battles in which lansquenets despoil each other or cut each other's throats, deserters hanging from trees with a raven greedily pecking out their eyes, plumed *cantinières*, standard-bearers swaggering along, proud and defiant, their chests thrown out, are his familiar themes; when he varies them, it is to make fun of dull-witted peasants or tell of anchorites' quarrels with demons who come to torment them in their hermitages. This jeering imagination that can jest at the horrors of life — the German "gallows-humor" — is the chief characteristic of Urs Graf's personality. Bitter and harrowing, his art is truly the mirror of an age given up to the bloody excesses of which the lansquenets were witnesses, and, on occasion, participants, in that democratic Switzerland where, with the impoverishment of the monasteries and churches whose commissions had guaranteed a livelihood to painters, there was only one resource left to those among them who practised the sole art tolerated by the iconoclasts — portraiture. Thus Holbein himself deemed it prudent to emigrate to England rather than become involved in the confusion of religious quarrels which had turned Basle into a tilting yard.

HANS HOLBEIN THE YOUNGER

Of all the painters in this uneasy century, weighed down, cluttered with the relics of medievalism and Gothic sensibility, Holbein is perhaps the only one who swiftly created a style of his own, as different from that of the Italians as from that of his Swabian, Franconian, Austrian or Swiss contemporaries. The spirit of the Renaissance blossomed out in him with a breadth and sureness of touch, no doubt the result of his association with the Basle humanists and Flemish or English men of letters whom he had the opportunity of meeting. Thus, to him the Renaissance is eminently a German affair, scarcely affected by the Italian spirit. For the same reason, the forms of the Lombardic Renaissance which he probably came across in the region of Milan where he is believed to have made a short journey, had only the slightest influence on his painting; his *Lais Corinthiaca* itself (1526, Basle) reminds us more of an Italianate painter of the Low Countries such as Metsys, Benson or Gossaert than an Italian known at first hand, despite a certain Leonardo atmosphere about the whole work. We may well believe that if he left his native town of Augsburg, it was in 1515 aged seventeen or eighteen when, justifiably enough, he aspired to aesthetic independence in order to escape from the supervision of his father who worked unashamedly in the Gothic tradition, and even from the influence of a Burgkmair.

We should be wrong however to regard these two Augsburg masters as artists of secondary rank, seeing they constitute the all-important hinge round which turned the transition from Gothic to the Renaissance in Swabia, Italian influence, the infusion of a new spirit in the small court of the Fugger family, in commercial and personal relations and "cultural exchanges" with the courts of the bankers, princes and *condottieri* of the Italian Peninsula.

Hans Burgkmair (1473-1531) had been a pupil of "Handsome Martin" Schongauer before he, like Dürer, had set off, about his seventeenth year, for his "tour of Northern Italy" which proved to be the wonder of his youth, and the fruits of which were to be consolidated by a longer stay, about fifteen years later (probably between 1506 and 1508). He was not however the man to depend on "foreigners"; all he consented to accept from them were lessons which could be integrated into his technique without encroaching on his personal idiom. The warm, golden light of Venetia, the brilliant color of his *St. John at Patmos* are an Italian contribution. The Flemish artists were equally in favor with Swabian bankers, and it is very possible that Burgkmair under their influence enriched that eclecticism with which his technique and aesthetics are equally imbued.

Ulrich Apt (circa 1481-1531), Leonhard Beck (circa 1480-1542), the artist whose monogram is L.S. (circa 1510-1540) and especially Jorg Breu (circa 1475-1537) reflect, with diverse fortunes and very varied means, different aspects of Swabian art at the beginning of the Renaissance.

To Breu is attributed a share of influence in the creation of the "Danubian" landscape school because of the background of his *Madonna and Child surrounded by Saints* (Berlin, 1512) which combines musical harmony with realism.

A similar eclecticism — though less Italianized — imbues the works of the Swabian masters who were contemporary with Burgkmair[12]. It was in that Augsburg ambience that the younger Holbein lived up to his twentieth year, and he learned a great deal; even among the old works of Burgkmair, the *Coronation of the Virgin* (Augsburg, 1507), the *Emperor Constantine and St. Sebastian* (Nuremberg, 1505) he found much he could borrow, and did not fail to do so; and he must have interrogated those tragic faces, truly permeated with an inner life and, in that, very different from the more conventional personages as from the archaic compositions of his father.

It is impossible to study the works of Holbein the Elder without noticing the discreet sensibility, honesty of mind, scrupulous talent with which he moved from the medievalism of the *Birth of the Virgin* of Augsburg Cathedral (1493) and the *Adoration of the Magi* of the Kaisheim Altar (Munich, 1502) to the fully fledged Renaissance works of his maturity or old age, the *Altarpiece of St. Sebastian* (Munich, 1516) for example, in which a tender delicacy of heart, Flemish in origin, is integrated with a feeling for decoration that is essentially Italian in spirit and expression.

Interested in spatial problems, Hans Holbein the Elder discovered ingenious solutions for relating the various areas of space in the same painting. In the panel of the *Beheading of St. Paul* (Augsburg), the figure of a woman, seen from the back, sitting on a chair listening to the sermon of the Apostle in the back part of the composition, connects the latter with the execution of St. Paul which is taking place in the foreground. This is by no means a medieval solution, for the painters of the fifteenth century were content to add episodes without troubling to connect them in the composition. The Renaissance décor with its classical colonnades of the room in which the *Annunciation* takes place, on the outer shutters of the *Altarpiece of St. Sebastian* (Munich), is likewise a manifestation of that modern spirit which exercised so powerful an influence on the artist's son. It will indeed be noted that the *Christ Bearing*

HANS HOLBEIN – THE AMBASSADORS. 1533 – (2,06; 2,09) NATIONAL GALLERY, LONDON

the Cross of Holbein the Younger (Karlsruhe) appears more archaic than the *Altar-piece of St. Sebastian* which it preceded only by one year.

Once Hans Holbein had shaken himself free from his father's supervision, he learned his job from the great Swiss decorators among whom the tradition of painted façades was at a high point; at Lucerne to start with, then at Basle. The considerable stylistic transformation which took place in his work between 1515, the date he left Augsburg, and his arrival at Basle in 1519, was perhaps reinforced by a journey to Lombardy of which nothing definite is known but which would explain a certain Leonardo influence in the *Zetter Virgin and Child* (Solothurn, 1522) and the hint of Mantegna in the *Dead Christ* of Basle (1521). The color has acquired a warmth lacking in his youthful works, which Holbein the Elder never had and which even in Burgkmair is an Italian borrowing. Holbein the Younger needed no Italian inspiration to confirm and increase his prodigious sense of monumental decoration with its fake architecture and trompe-l'œil such as are to be found in his Basle frescoes, those of the *House of the Dance* and the Rathaus. Teutonic and Latin society were in close touch with each other in Basle, thanks to the Humanists who lived in that highly cultured town. It was in Basle that some years before, his elder brother, Ambrosius (1493-between 1519 and 1526) whom a precocious talent and early death invest with a sense of tragedy, had settled. The portrait of *Johannes Herbster*, painted by Ambrosius in 1516, immortalized Holbein's elder son and his almost forgotten master who fought in Italy with the Basle militia, and, despite his bellicose life, died as late as 1550 — of the Plague, if tradition be true — at the age of over eighty.

It was in the humanist ambience of Boniface Amerbach, Erasmus, Froben, Beatus Rhenanus, that Holbein cultivated his taste for reflection, meditation, classical texts and the curiosity about men's inner life that he was to bring to the surface in his magnificent portraits. He did not neglect the best examples and most useful lessons, since he frequented the monastery of Isenheim where his father lived the last years of his life and where he had long enjoyed familiarity with the Matthias Grünewald Altarpiece. He also got to know the French Renaissance in the course of a journey in Touraine and Berry. This French journey took place in 1524, a period when the violent clashes between opposing religious sects made a stay in Basle difficult for an artist who claimed to be living "above the struggle". We may assume that the young artist went off to try and find employment in the service of the French king, and it was probably his failure to do so that stimulated him to try a second chance two years later in England, with what success we know. A letter from Erasmus served as an effective introduction to English Humanists, especially to Thomas More.

"The arts are freezing here", the author of the *Eulogy of Madness* had written in a letter to Peter Aegidius. Portraitist of Erasmus and warmly praised by that philosopher for his work, Holbein possessed all the qualities which commended him to a refined, cultivated society of men among whom the new ideas sharpened that curiosity concerning the character and soul which distinguished Holbein from all his contemporaries. Having acclimatized himself in London, where — except for a few short stays in Basle, probably in connection with business matters — he was to remain until his death in 1543, Holbein became Henry VIII's court painter and the favourite portraitist of the English nobility whose calm and haughty distinction he has so magnificently expressed.

We are perfectly justified in considering Holbein's portraits as among the finest and most faithful which have ever been painted. Even if we take into account the tendency towards the grotesque which characterizes the engraved series, the *Dance of Death*, and the funereal anamorphism of the *Ambassadors* (London) with the macabre symbol hidden in the form of a picturesque enigma, the essential character of Holbein's personality is the powerful and scrupulous objectivity of the portraits of *Sieur de Morette* (Dresden), the *Duke of Norfolk* (Windsor Castle), the *Royal Falconer, Robert Cheseman* (The Hague 1533), *Sir Thomas Godsalve* (Dresden), *George Gisse* (Berlin, 1532), the *Unknown Young Man* of Berlin (1541); all these faces seem weighed down with sadness, disillusion, the *taedium vitae*, in a stillness which has something sinister about it. What psychological insight reveals here is not only an undefined anguish, peculiar to the men of a period when the morrow must always be precarious and whom danger perpetually besets, but furthermore that vague awareness of the fleeting nature and the continual threats of life even in the midst of apparent security. In Germany, the cruel wars of the Reformation and the brutal massacres — on every hand — in the Peasants' Wars; in England, the implacable and hypocritical caprices of Henry VIII who in Holbein's portraits appears less "wild" than in Shakespeare, but no less dangerous.

The curiosity about the human soul however, stops at this point, that is at a certain depth beyond which the artist will not or cannot commit himself. The atmosphere of the English court which he scarcely left between 1526 and 1543, that is for almost two decades, dictated the same imperatives as it had to Hilliard, Sir Peter Lely or Kneller, that is a more or less superficial psychology, characteristic of those sitters who have no objection to surrendering their face to the painter but refuse him access to their inner being. Doubtless Hans Holbein's very nature accommodated itself to these "reserves," without too much difficulty, and he lacked the impetuosity to violate the secrets of his sitters' lives which drove Dürer to engage in a veritable battle with his model until the latter "came into the open"; it is at that stage that Holbein, by way of compensation, acquires that kind of magic reality, impassioned vehemence with which he seizes hold of the spectator in his turn and dominates and completely possesses him.

It sometimes seems that the tactile factor of flesh, a piece of cloth, a jewel, has as much value, that is "plastic" value, as the psychological element. Holbein's personages scrupulously suppress all those things about themselves that Dürer brings out. It would be extremely difficult to find a truly Faustian portrait among his works, to such an extent is dissimulation considered wise and prudent even among men who probably have little to hide. The temperament of the painter is responsible for this habit characteristic of Holbein society of advancing behind a mask (*larvatus prodeo*, as Descartes puts it). The mask which the painter places over his model's feature, is his own, assumed through excessive discretion perhaps, or by way of precaution against not taking more than he is giving. Because of this, these portraits, admirable though they are, are less satisfying than those of Dürer and the latter's Faustian progeny. Thus, Holbein was lacking in that German "constant," so much its characteristic from medieval sculpture to Expressionism and so accurately described in Dagobert Frey's phrase the "daemon of the eye."

In this German sixteenth century which includes perhaps the finest portraits done anywhere during that period — and there were, as I am well aware, Clouet and Matsys, and Josse van Cleve, and Scorel and Raphael — we can clearly distinguish two parallel streams which we cannot define more precisely than by saying that one is Holbein's, the other Dürer's. This definition allows us to classify those among the extremely numerous artists of this uneasy century who belong to the school of Holbein, more concerned with formal expression than emotion, which thrusts tragedy back into the depths of the consciousness, instead of permitting it to show in the facial expression, which contents itself with a certain "superficiality," seizes hold of the "being" of an individual and not his potentiality. The other category associated with Dürer and his followers, the disturbed and anxious Faustian painters, do not weigh up their sitter in a moment but take in his whole life, not as revealed in the visible, narrowly circumscribed personality but in the obscure regions of the ego of which the sitter himself is ignorant and which the painter has to snatch from the shadows as through a magic incantation.

THE GERMAN PORTRAIT IN THE SIXTEENTH CENTURY

With the Renaissance, the knowledge of individual character, physical peculiarities and psychology became the raw material of the kind of portraiture which had already made a discreet beginning during the preceding century. Portraits of "donors" were painted with energetic emphasis, self-portraits of artists had found their way into the crowds in Biblical episodes, but it was not until the second half of the fifteenth century that the individualized and extremely personalized portrait begins to count in its own right. The rise of the Middle Class and the bankers favored this art of portraiture, to which the iconoclastic attitude of the Reformation, hostile to religious art, was to give a considerable stimulus. Just as man replaced God at the center of the universe in the philosophy of the Humanists, the ban on "image-making" brought about the replacement of the pious picture not by mythological scenes which were still foreign to Germany as a whole, but by the accurate representation of reality. And as there is no more interesting study for man than man himself, the representation of the exterior and inner being soon became a matter of primary importance. In proportion to the superficiality or depth of this curiosity the portraiture is decorative and formal, or conversely, dramatic, since the fate of the individual can be read in his portrait.

The classification that was made of "types," "characters," the sketching-out of a systematic and dogmatic physiognomy, lent a new interest to these representations which were not prompted by mere vanity. The portrait as an instrument of knowledge played an all-important rôle in the sixteenth century, and we can understand why humanist circles favored and encouraged its practice; it was Erasmus' acknowledgment of the quality of his portrait painted by Holbein that recommended him to his English friends and, incidentally, made the artist's fortune.

At no other period in Germany, not even in the eighteenth century, were there so many portrait painters; and we note that when these artists were also painters of altarpieces or easel pictures, it was in their portrait work that they were most modern and abreast of their times.

We have just suggested a system of dividing sixteenth century portraits into those of people as they are, with Holbein as their principal exponent, and portraits of potentiality, represented in the front rank by Dürer. It is not a classification to apply too rigorously or systematically; the sole aim behind it is to separate the two main trends, granted, of course, that we could likewise speak of the court portrait and the formal portrait, but in that case we should no longer be considering the portrait as a source of knowledge and the expression of the world within[13].

Lucas Cranach the Younger (1515-1586), like his brother Hans, was resigned for a long time to working in his father's workshop which was a veritable picture factory, and he effaced his personality to such an extent that it is difficult to sort out his share in the work of Lucas Cranach the Elder. In his portraits on the other hand (*Portrait of Leonhard Badehorn*, Berlin), he gave himself up to his own character, consented to be himself, and we believe we can also recognize his hand in two studio works, a *Portrait of a Woman* and a *Portrait of a Man* which owe nothing to the mannered and sometimes ironic elegance of his father. A kind of melancholy ruggedness, an almost peasant simplicity leads us to suppose that Cranach the Younger tried his hand out on these before achieving the success of the Badehorn portrait.

It could be said of the Swabian Christoph Amberger (circa 1500-1561) that he comes closest to Holbein and is the most worthy of comparison with him; he, too, studied Burgkmair, got to know the Venetian painters on the spot, frequented the Fuggers' Palazzo, admired their truly European collection in which Spanish and Portuguese masters hung side by side with those from Flanders and France. He met Charles V and painted a portrait of him without achieving more than a superficial result, almost comic in the expression of extreme stupidity which he attributed to the Emperor, while in the same gallery we can admire the look of high and clear intelligence, the dignity of the Humanist, of the "scholar" in his portrait of the Augsburg cosmographer, *Sebastian Munster*, with the *Portrait of a Prince* (Augsburg, 1523), his best work — and several portraits of the Mörz and Fugger families that belong to private collections in Swabia. More than his religious paintings and façade decorations, Amberger's court portraits of the great Augsburg bankers who by their loans of money to kings, the Emperor and the Pope had insinuated themselves into the complex workings of European politics, made him the rival and — though less successful — the equal of Erasmus' friend.

Among the great "romantics" of this restless time, that is to say those who were fascinated by the problems of their sitters' potentiality rather than their present "being," Dürer's spiritual heirs and disturbed by the same doubts, were those artists for whom the model is not merely the man of the immediate present, the psychological enigma which everybody represents to everybody else. Among these we are not surprised to encounter the strange artist Baldung Grien with two extremely curious portraits — the *Graf von Loewenstein* (Berlin 1513) and the mysterious *Count Palatine Philip the Warrior* (Munich, 1517). The uneasy, almost worried expression we catch in the eyes of these men whom the artist has sounded to the depths of their souls, is completely in the tradition of the *Hercules strangling Antaeus* in Cassel and the *Death* of Basle. And what we thought of the complex nature of the "green painter" is confirmed by the most revealing works any artist can pass down to us — portraits.

From this point of view, it is fitting that we should consider alongside Baldung a very little known painter, Lucas Furtnagel, who worked in Augsburg in Hans Burgkmair's circle and to whom nowadays we attribute the portrait of *Hans Burgkmair and his Wife* (Vienna, 1529). This famous panel portrays, as we know, the painter and his wife, Anna Allerlahn, aged respectively 57 and 52, looking into a mirror in which two skulls are reflected, while the inscription of the picture makes this macabre comment, "This is what we both were but in the mirror it was something very different..."

This *memento mori* is a frequent theme at a time when congregations had the dance of death painted in churches and monastery cloisters and representations of Death engraved by Holbein and Dürer on their tables; even in the formal portrait of the wealthy *Young Patrician* of Basle, already mentioned, painted by Master H.F., behind this flourishing figure of the young man Death appears, brandishing his hour-glass. This moral lesson, valid and eloquent as it is at all times, assumed a particular significance through the fact that just at that time the Germanic countries were caught up in the horrors of religious strife and the atrocities of the Peasants' Wars. When Arnold Böcklin took up the theme at the end of the nineteenth century in a self-portrait in which we see him before his easel while a skeleton peers over his shoulder to see what he is painting, it is the gloomy evocation of Baroque melancholy already present in the sixteenth century which was to last up to the post-Romantic of *The Plague* (Basle).

This same macabre note is to be found again in the work of the two brothers, Tom Ring, of Münster — Ludwig (1530-1584) and Hermann (1520-1597). In the central panel of a *Last Judgment* (Utrecht), the figure of Death, sitting on a coffin is aiming an arrow, not in the direction of the people in the picture but straight at the spectator, the direct target of this cruel threat. The two brothers, like their father, Ludger Tom Ring (1496-1547), rank among the most remarkable fantastic painters of a period which was infatuated with the supernatural, and are at the same time excellent portraitists. There is a fine portrait of his wife, *Anna Rorup* (1540) by Ludger in Cologne; of the young Hermann we have a *Portrait of a Stranger*, calmer, less obviously anxious but shuddering, so to speak, with inner uneasiness (Berlin).

The skull of the "vanities," the discreet warning, drawing attention to the famous "Hodie mihi," appears again in the *Portrait of a Man* by Martin Schaffner (Berlin); the sitter does not look at it — it is unnecessary, the memento mori being in the forefront of all his thoughts — he merely points a finger at it, while the sad gravity of the face underlines the significance of this meditation on the ultimate end. In the whole corpus of his portraits, the Swabian Martin Schaffner (c. 1480 - c. 1547), comes before us as an observant and painstaking realist, an eclectic who has learned from the Italians no less than from Dürer, Schaüffelein and Burgkmair; the *Portrait of Eitel Besserer on a Gold Background* (Ulm Cathedral, 1510), with his hirsute beard and fur cap, seems a concession to the anecdotal, but this depiction of an old man, limned, one might say, by care, age and fatigue, telling his beads with noble dignity, is a pathetic figure, comparable to the Berlin *Man with the Skull.* Of all the Swabian school he is beyond all doubt the most dramatic — that is, in his portraiture — much more than the productive and attractive Bernhard Strigel (circa 1460-1528) in the background of whose famous *Portrait of the Rehlingen Family* (Munich, 1517) we discover an exquisite landscape, much more interesting in itself than the crowd of the Rehlingen children, uninspiring in expression and — to all appearances — terrorized by a pitiless father; whereas the *Family of the Emperor Maximilian* (Vienna) is more like an odd assembly of caricatures. The fashionable elegance of the Swabian towns nevertheless found a painstaking and faithful historiographer in Strigel at a period when, as the popular adage had it: "Venice power; Augsburg magnificence; Nuremberg wit; Strasburg arms; Ulm money..."

The excellence of portraiture in Cologne is represented above all by an enigmatic, subtle and disturbing figure of an *Unknown Woman*, painted by the Master of the Legend of St. Ursula about the year 1500; by the amazing *Warrior*, accoutred in a suit of armor which transforms him into a gigantic scarab, shining and proud, by Master L.S. (Berlin), and by the prolific dynasty of the Bruyns, as famed for their religious as for their portrait painting. They are thought to have been of Netherlandish stock, for it is the characteristics of Low Country painting that predominate in the works of Barthel the Elder (1493-circa 1555) and his son Barthel Bruyn the Younger (circa 1550-before 1610), rather than the tradition of Cologne to which these, perhaps recent, immigrants seem alien. In their paintings however we can point to great beauties and, in particular, to figures of considerable liveliness.

It is very difficult to say at what precise moment German painting began to be Baroque, for in Germany a kind of permanent Baroque spirit exists. What we *can* say is that the Renaissance itself presented very few of the classical characteristics to be found in France and Italy, and that in Germany the Baroque was immediately integrated into Gothic. Everything that is classical, on the other hand, is imported, and comes either from Italy or Flanders — themselves Italianized. If the classical ideal therefore appears alien to German art, Baroque, like Gothic, is one of the richest and most characteristic manifestations of its genius; this, despite the fact that the majority of German Baroque painters learned the idiom at the Schools of Venice, Naples or Rome.

Ought we to distinguish between Baroque and Rococo elements with different aspirations and forms in German painting of the seventeenth and eighteenth centuries? Certainly not. It may be extremely difficult to decide exactly when Baroque first begins in the Renaissance ambience from which it emanated, but it is more difficult still to put one's finger on the transition period when Baroque moved into Rococo as into something new and different.

In Germany, Rococo is like a new state of Baroque, *a new way of being Baroque.* All we can do is to take the Baroque period and distinguish in it various periods, beginning with that when the Baroque spirit contaminated and agitated Renaissance forms; this is chiefly evident in the decorations with fantastically contorted, intertwined and twisted arabesques, which led up to the religious Baroque of the Counter-Reformation and ended with the idyllic and hedonistic Baroque which justifies the appellation, Rococo.

The most important thing where Baroque painting is concerned is to distinguish between imported elements and those which spring from German sources. In other words, the foreign elements introduced from Rome on the one hand, and on the other, everything that was roused and set in motion by the Baroque "constant" which has its origin in spiritual unrest. Thus Baroque became a new way of conceiving both the individual man and the universe, and representing them with those plastic and pictorial means capable of expressing passion and emotion in their pure state, in that great dramatic tide of which the fused colors of a Maulbertsch, the rapid and contrasted rhythms of an Asam are the most curious and significant manifestations.

The two countries which exercised a strong attraction on the German artists of this first Baroque phase, which runs from the end of the sixteenth to the first half of the seventeenth century, are Holland and Italy. The political and religious disorders caused by the Reformation had rent the country asunder, involved the propertied classes in poverty and distress and destroyed that rich source of art which the churches and monasteries represented on the spiritual side. In such circumstances it was natural that the painters should look elsewhere for a more favorable atmosphere. The result of this migration was, first and foremost, that the essentially Germanic character of sixteenth century art was complicated by foreign contributions. In the process of their initiation into an aesthetic system different from that which had been handed down to them by tradition, they opened their minds to ways of thought, feeling and expression which at first seemed alien but which they quickly assimilated and transformed sufficiently to create something of vigorous originality. The foreign countries, for their part, received and accepted the German artists with that open and generous liberalism which always favours eclecticism and learned from them perhaps as much as they imparted. The most striking example of this "creative eclecticism," associating as it does Italy and Holland with Germany as the intermediary, is provided by Adam Elsheimer (1578-1620).

Of purely German stock, Elsheimer found a natural place in sixteenth century German painting through his master, Philipp Uffenbach (1566-1636), a former pupil of Grimmer who in his turn had been the pupil of Nithardt-Grünewald. Furthermore, he had been introduced to landscape painting by a painter from Frankenthal, Peter Schouibroeck, a disciple of the Fleming, Coninxloo. Elsheimer's art was composite even in its early manifestations, and it became more so when this man, whom the men of Rome were to call "Adamo Tedesco" and who was to die in the Eternal City at the youthful age of thirty-two, settled in Italy in the last years of the century.

In Venice Elsheimer studied Tintoretto particularly, in Rome Caravaggio and the realists of chiaroscuro. The light-effects for which he was to become famous and which suffuse scenes of inward tranquillity with mysterious poetry and nocturnal landscapes, transfigured by a pale moon and faint fires, had already captivated painters of preceding generations, and Altdorfer, in particular had excelled in them. For Elsheimer, however, as for his predecessors, above all those of the Danube School, the landscape is in itself a lyrical element. You only needed to listen to the voices of the Panic forces that resided there to release their hidden music. The Roman Campagna was transfigured in Elsheimer's work as it was in that of Claude Lorrain, by that surrealist interpretation of the real which pursues the spirit of things beyond their visible appearance. The *Burning of Troy* of Munich, the Dresden *Flight into Egypt* and the Munich version, painted the year before his death, the *David* and *St. Christopher* of Berlin, both of which are sometimes disputed, fittingly represent the various aspects of Elsheimer's art. In the last two pictures mentioned, he pastiches Caravaggio without however resorting to slavish imitation. More sober than the realism of the Naples or Bologna schools, "Adamo Tedesco's" has a discretion and reserve and an avoidance of effect which are his special characteristics. He is never theatrical even when the lighting effects in his paintings remind one of the stage.

Elsheimer is in point of fact free from that affectation inseparable from truly Mannerist art. The *Landscape with Nymphs Bathing*, of Berlin, with its harmonious partition of the masses of foliage between light and shadow, the hidden tranquillity of his lake, forbidden to human beings, the reflections of the setting sun on the rounded hills, seems a kind of incantation, a secret appeal addressed to the elemental forces; the naked woman rising from the water resembles those Giorgione figures who epitomize the whole life of nature and, as it were, re-constitute it, adding to it the mystery of human beings and gods.

Elsheimer never deliberately took Giorgione for his model whereas he admitted to admiring the Carracci and Caravaggio. But his true master was the painter of Castelfranco, just as his real pupil is Rembrandt. When we compare his early work

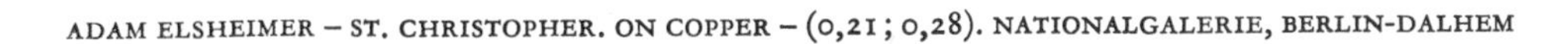

ADAM ELSHEIMER – ST. CHRISTOPHER. ON COPPER – (0,21; 0,28). NATIONALGALERIE, BERLIN-DALHEM

GERMAN SCHOOL – CUPBOARD WITH BOTTLES AND BOOKS. CIRCA 1470-1480
(1,06; 0,81) – MORTIMER BRANDT GALLERY, NEW YORK

with those executed during the dozen years of the Roman period, we are struck by the metarmorphosis which came about when he was in contact with Latin soil. Elsheimer blossomed out in those dozen years because he needed precisely that contact before he could come to a full realization of his powers and become what he was during the Roman period, namely — and to the great benefit of all the Dutch artists who knew him — one of the most fruitful points of departure of the painting of the Netherlands in the seventeenth century [14].

Whether it was a question of landscape, portraits or genre painting, these emigrant Teutons docilely followed the path marked out for them by foreign painters. It may have been that there no longer existed in the Germany of that time an ambience capable of capturing and inspiring these artists, it may have been the lure of the great artistic capitals, Amsterdam, Venice and Rome that proved irresistible to the Germans making their European tour and held them fast. The fact remains that these Germans figured frequently in the "foreign legion" of Flanders, Holland and Italy where they found honorable niches, paying for the hospitality accorded them with useful samples of their art, which always retained some element of their national genius.

This it particularly so in the case of the still life, which is not indigenous in German painting, since the Germans while cherishing the reality of the object, fail to separate it from its human context. At no period in its artistic history did Germany endow the still life with that autonomous character which it enjoys in France, Holland or Spain. We must therefore attribute a foreign origin to the still life object paintings of Georg Flegel, for example, whose *Still Life with Candle* (Karlsruhe) has collected all the ingredients of "vanity" in the Dutch vein. Moravian by birth, Flegel (1563-1638) appears to have been the pupil of the Flemish artist, Soreau, through whom he is connected with another famous still life painter, the Alsatian, Sebastian Stosskopff (1597-1657).

Those two artists, linked, albeit tenuously, by the fact that they concerned themselves with a genre seldom practiced in German painting, are very different. Georg Flegel is a realist whose special concern is the tactile truth of substances and the architecture of assemblages of objects based on an almost abstract principle of construction. His paint has the rich, supple and warm consistency of the Dutch practitioners, the intriguing reflections of lighted candles which we encounter in the Italian Baschenis and the French painter Baugin. Sometimes he moves in the direction of metaphysical thought; then the allusion to death, the vanity of all things, effects, as it were, its own release from a collection of objects, each of which repeats in its own fashion its own *memento mori*. But Flegel is no metaphysician; merely a skilled and brilliant painter, sensitive to the special quality each substance offers to the eye, ear or touch. Less sensual — or sensorial — than the Dutch, his concern is more with the interplay of volumes; his still lifes appeal to the intellect as much as, if not more than to the senses.

In that, he is very different from another famous painter of still lifes, Abraham Mignon (1640-1679), a pupil of De Heem and a specialist in sumptuous bouquets and in strange settings in which insects, mice and snakes move about among thistles and fungi.

A native of Strasburg, that meeting place of the Teutonic and Latin-Celtic world, Stosskopff owes less to the Dutch than Mignon or even Flegel does. His conception of the *memento mori* finds its natural expression in the weird and striking image of a basket containing crystal glasses of extreme fragility, some of which are broken. The moralizing spirit of "vanity" could have no more telling image.

It is the same spirit of moralizing "vanities" that dictates the subject to a native of Hamburg, Johann Georg Hainz, the fine *Jewel Cupboard* of the Kunsthalle at Hamburg (1666). The picture shows those rare and precious objects which rich and inquisitive collectors assembled in their Wunderkammer — a skull appears on one of the shelves, less as a curiosity than a warning to the spectator of the fragility of the chased goblets, carved ivories, jewels which are next to it and of the brief span of life left to the possessor of these wonders.

Also from Hamburg, that other composer of still lifes, Heinrich Stravius (? -1690) whose major preoccupation was with illusionist representation, was scrupulously accurate in reproducing specimens of game hanging from the wall exactly as the huntsmen had hung them on their return. His detail comes extremely near to trompe-l'œil.

Baroque religious painting inspired two easel artists who share the distinctive feature of having taken vows and become monks without having abandoned their painting. They are M. L. Wildmann (1630-1706) and C.A. Ruthardt (1630-1703). The sacred element, however, is not the distinguishing feature of either; they are, first and foremost, landscape and animal painters and of no great originality in their interpretation of themes familiar to the Dutch and Flemings [15].

DECORATION ON THE GRAND SCALE

SACRED AND PROFANE

The Baroque decoration of palaces, churches and religious foundations in Germany, Austria and Switzerland surprises us first by its sheer profusion. There are some three to four thousand huge ensembles painted in fresco, involving ninety artists of the first order, aided by hundreds of assistants and apprentices (Tintelnot); Feulner, for his part, has noted one thousand nine hundred important Baroque ensembles in Swabia and Bavaria alone. This extraordinary proliferation of an art form which is *the* characteristic means of Baroque expression, reveals to us that at this time — that is, from the seventeenth century to the end of the eighteenth, over the scattered area covered by Teutonic painting which also extends as far as Bohemia and Hungary — there existed a society which felt the desire and need for these glorious and fantastic decorations.

This state of mind, which is something more than an aesthetic outlook, was favored too by the presence of great architects, Dietzenhofer, Penz, Fischer von Erlach, Neumann, Hildebrandt, whose style called for the collaboration of sculptors, stucco-painters and painters. There was no shortage of sculptors nor of stucco-painters, of whom there existed a famous School at Wessobrun and whose skill, imagination and talent rivalled that of the Italians. The buildings which were of amazing splendor benefited from the lavishness of princes who vied with each other in luxury and taste in the construction and decoration of their palaces, and also from the wealth of the bishoprics, abbeys and monasteries, and furthermore from the tendency of the high church dignitaries — themselves not infrequently of high rank — to imitate the princes, even to the point of introducing purely profane elements into their work. We can be forgiven for noting with some surprise the extent to which certain conventual libraries — intended one might suppose as places for study and contemplation — are covered with a decoration that is almost extravagantly lavish and elaborate. As for churches, in Catholic provinces of the Germanic countries they are clothed in a magnificence directed at the senses and the sensiblity and, with an unprecedented display of beauty and opulence — unrivalled outside the Byzantine churches — proclaim the glory of God and the saints. The spirit of the Counter-Reformation had encouraged this excess and even this abuse of adornment in religious buildings. The aim was to arouse a kind of *spiritual surrealism* (Tintelnot) with a tendency towards illusionism in which the visionary world was mingled with the world of reality. This illusionism which caused ceilings to melt away behind the supernatural glory of the Madonna or a saint, substituted light for matter; it dematerialized objects, and by means of perspective devices analogous to those used in the theatre suggested the presence of an infinite space in which the imagination, unimpeded by any obstacle, prolonged its dreams and visions.

The close association, in a unity of spirit and homogeneity of creation, of different categories of artists participating in the construction and decoration of the Baroque edifice, gives the latter a total harmony to which, for full measure, is added music whose forms and structure are of the same nature as those of architecture, sculpture, painting and stucco. The return to the fresco as a technique of decorative expression is codified in the celebrated work by Werner, a picturesque and learned treatise, based on a wealth of practical experience, published in Erfurt in 1781. It represented for the second period of Baroque painting — which we may call Rococo — what Cennini represents for the Renaissance in Italy.

From the sixteenth century on, the decorated façades which were numerous at this period (Holbein's at Basle, Stimmer's at Schaffhausen, Kager's at Augsburg) present an originality of spatial construction and plastic expression which is more and more consolidated during the seventeenth century with Johann Paul Schor (1615-1674), Johann Joseph Waldmann (†1712), Michael Wildmann (1630-1706), who followed Hans Werle, Christoph Schwarz and Melchior Bocksberger. The church of St. Joseph at Grüssau (1695) by Wildmann, is completely free of any Italian influence despite its intense Baroque idiom. Wildmann makes room both for the lyrical and naturalistic landscape; and this was to remain one of the dominant characteristics of German Baroque.

This German Baroque, so personal, so individual in style, which pursued its course of development and elaboration all through the seventeenth century, delving into itself, enriching its means of expression and intensifying its spirit, was already, as the new century dawned, in full possession of its ideals and had a perfect command of techniques for creating imaginary perspectives which "burst" through walls and ceilings and left an unbridled imagination free to wander in complete independence. These painters had not lost the sense of the real. They transported and transposed it in the composition which is at the same time of a superterrestrial, visionary and theatrical reality, served by a powerful orchestration of dynamic forms and brilliant colors, just as in the realm of music the symphony orchestra is enriched by the addition of new instruments. The collaboration of architect, painter and sculptor becomes even closer than in the preceding century. The best example of this is to be found in the Asam family in which all these arts were practiced with genius. "The painting of the artist Cosmas begins at the point where architectural possibilities are exhausted, and the resources of the sculptor Egid come into play at the moment when worlds of illusionist fresco and the existentialist space of the spectator must be merged into one single entity" (Tintelnot). Thus it comes about that Hans Georg Asam (1649-1711) and his two sons, Egid Quirin and Cosmas Damian (1686-1739) — the one whom we find of most interest since he is "the painter of the family" — constitute the ideal workshop of the Baroque period in its harmonious completeness.

A Baroque church such as Sankt Johannes von Nepomuk in Munich (1733) offers a unity of style which arises from the fact that the Asam brothers designed the plan, undertook the construction and decoration, and thus gave the edifice, which has the contour of a violin, a harmony comparable to that obtained by a symphony orchestra, in which voices and sounds blend perfectly even when they are not in unison. Cosmas Damian, the painter brother of the group, had received the Accademia di San Luca award in Rome in 1713. Later he made the acquaintance of Rubens' works which he found profoundly impressive, but — Italian or Flemish — these borrowings were quickly assimilated into an extremely original conception of space, built up on those fantastic perspective devices such as we see in the ceiling of the monastic church of Weingarten (1717), and in the Jakobskirche, Innsbrück, which create the illusion of colonnades, superimposed and stretching away into the distance until they encounter the place where the fake void in the cupola opens into the sky. Later, in the conventual church of Wahlstatt (1731), at Kladrau (1726), at Sankt Emmeran in Regensburg (1732), these pieces of closed architecture give way to aerial compositions which have free play in a contourless space. It follows this pattern in the very Rubens-like ceiling of the Knights' Hall in the castle of Mannheim (1730) and in that of the castle of Alteglofsheim. (1729).

Contrary to what was formerly claimed, there are important differences between the religious art of Cosmas Damian Asam and his lay decorations. The eloquent virtuosity with which he treated pious themes, their dramatic pathos and his frequent recourse to emotional idioms, not unlike those we associate with the theatre, all these elements nevertheless preserve a secret virtue of their own, and the melody of colors, comparable to that of musical instruments, celebrates the majesty of God and the glory of the saints with true sincerity.

If nowadays the great Baroque ensembles leave us with the impression that all the lines, the thrusts towards the center and the roof were combined in such a way as to carry the pictorial decoration of the vault or ceiling to its highest intensity, it must not be forgotten that forceful architectural personalities of real genius, such as Mungengast, Prandauer, Fischer, Neumann, Hildebrandt made it incumbent on the painters to conform to an idiom of expression of which the bare building was already both the "support", vehicle and the exhibitor. The strict need to "cling" to the architecture on the part of these painters — trained for the most part in Italy — led to the preponderance of their German genius over their Latin acquisitions.

This is, in fact, what happened to Asam and also to Johann Michael Rottmayr (1654-1730) who had worked in a Venetian studio for fifteen years. There he had acquired his mastery of the *sotto in su* perspective problem for which he discovers ingenious solutions in his frescoes in the castle of Frain (1696) and above all in the Sankt Mathiaskirche in Breslau (1704-1706), which is his great triumph. Rottmayr is not so much of a musician as Asam, more concerned as he probably was with plastic problems which he resolved with less naturalness. Daniel Gran (1694-1757) had also been at the Italian School — Solimena's at Naples, Ricci's at Venice. The work most representative of his clear, cogent thought, the "order" which controls his complex patterns of spiral rhythms, is the ceiling of the National Library of Vienna (1730). His compositions are very airy, the groups of people being harmoniously disposed among the clouds where children disport themselves.

Despite his Italian name and his ancestry (Neapolitan in all probability), Bartholomäus Altomonte (1707-1774) belongs essentially to Austrian Baroque. The *Triumph of the Church* which he painted in 1750 in the conventual church of Wilhering, near Linz, his frescoes of the Herzogenburg Library and the curious, architectural-like vistas of Spital am Pyhrn (1741), offer a profusion of attractive details among a host of celestial personages, arranged somewhat as a classical hierarchy.

Liberty of style, the possibility of making a completely free choice from the amazing repertory of plastic and pictorial means that Baroque puts at the artist's disposal, stimulate the caprice and unfettered expression of each painter's unique and most individual contribution. The almost romantic landscape paintings of the Hamburg artist, Johann Oswald Harms (1643) at Salzdahlum, exploit the fantastic and mysterious elements in Baroque nature. Paul Troger (1698-1762) painted theatre *décor* in Vienna; few cupolas are as vigorous as that of the church of Altenburg am Kamp (1733) in which the figures sweep on with an irresistible violence in a series of concentric circles until they reach the illusory cupola-lantern; it is as if a tempest blast were blowing through the realm of the Blessed. At Zwiefallen (1738), Franz Jozef Spiegler skilfully merges imaginary architecture in the eddies of the clouds, and thereby suggests that typically Baroque phenomenon, the metamorphosis of matter, the penetration by light of opaque and heavy substances which in their turn become etherialized, transparent and almost defy gravity.

Christoph Thomas Scheffler (1699-1756) who belonged to a famous family of Swabian artists, adopted a very different but no less striking and still more fantastic line in his painting of the nave of Sankt Paulin of Trier, representing the *Triumph of the Cross.* Scheffler frames scenes in which the Holy Cross is exalted by a setting of rocky cliffs of tortured shapes which look as though they had been thrown up by a volcanic eruption; voids which are luminous pierce these granite blocks, which are almost fused with the stucco reliefs capriciously distorted and are transformed into clouds as if by some mysterious incantation.

JOHANN WOLFGANG BAUMGARTNER – AMERICA. SKETCH. 1750 – (0,255; 0,38) MUSEUM, AUGSBURG

Another phenomenon characteristic of this second wave of the Baroque period which we may call Rococo, is the increasing importance given to landscape elements. Trompe-l'œil buildings are not suppressed but opened up to reveal woods, prospects of trees. The romanticism which we have already noted in the Harms, blossomed out further in Johann Georg Bergmüller (1688-1762) who had a similar predilection for picturesque details and amused himself by building a trompe-l'œil masons' scaffolding and a stone masons' yard in the frescoes of the nave of Steingaden (1740). In this work he rivals that virtuoso of illusion, Melchior Steidl († 1727) whose frescoes in the Residenz at Bamberg and the monastery at Sankt Florian renewed the aerial colonnades of Andrea Pozzo, at the same time adding a richly fabulous and purely irrational element which transforms the Cyclopean architecture into dream figures.

As Rococo fantasy and the wit that accompanied it dominated great decoration more and more, the distinction between sacred and profane art became less pronounced. The energetic spiritual impulse of the first Baroque period lost its seriousness and profundity. The theatrical elements, already numerous but restricted to tragic expression, now turned towards the idyllic. The pagan divinities with their sensual graces were preferred to martyrs and anchorites, and we might almost believe that in certain abbeys and churches love of the world without had almost effaced more pious preoccupations. A virtuoso of profane decoration such as Johann Baptist Zimmermann (1680-1758) opens up dream-parks for us in the castle of Nymphenburg. But if we study the frescoes in the church of Steinhausen (1731), which preceded those of Nymphenburg by twenty-six years, we already see the melodious fountains, avenues of poplar trees, forest edges reminiscent of pagan paradises. Like Tiepolo and so many other Baroque decorators, Zimmermann had a partiality for the *Four Quarters of the World*, a theme which under the pretext of celebrating the universal Marian cult or the adoration of Apollo, exploited the pictorial resources of local color, tentatively discovered by the seventeenth century and splendidly amplified in the eighteenth.

Christian Winck (1738-1797), a brilliant and facile painter and a rich colorist, with his typical Bavarian familiarity, evidently enjoyed introducing villagers who can be recognized in their everyday tasks and apparel in his church decorations.

In the eighteenth century Augsburg possessed a school of painters comparable in quality to the school it had possessed in the seventeenth. Three major personalities can be distinguished among the immense number of talented decorators — Johann Evangelist Holzer (1709-1740), Tyrolese by birth who never lost his peasant vigor, a simple, sometimes even humorous sincerity. Holzer is most of all a realist, and his personages are taken from life; his saints, like farm-workers (Church of St. Anthony at Partenkirchen, 1736), his chubby-cheeked children and his peasant girls do not however look too much out of place in their setting of trompe-l'œil architecture, illuminated like scenes in a tragedy. Johann Wolfgang Baumgartner, who is also a Swabian, roughs out (1756-1759) the episodes of the *Discovery of the Cross* at Bergen, near Augsburg on curious geometric bases. A man of Augsburg by adoption, though not by birth, Gottfried Bernhard Gös (1708-1774) decorated the conventual church of Birnau on Lake Constance with charm and magnificence in a fairly traditional style. Franz Martin Kuen (1719- ?) a pupil of Bergmüller, on the other hand, renewed the Rococo *décor* with wings in pure Rocaille style, rising among the foliage of a park such as we see in the luxurious and pagan library in the monastery of Wiblingen.

With Johann Baptist Enderle (1725-1798), greatly influenced by Van Dyck and Tiepolo conjointly — strange bedfellows — with Johann Anwanders (1715-1770), most of all with Matthias Günther (1705-1788), who represents the climax of Rococo in South Germany, we become aware of an eclecticism which gives the decorative orchestration of the fresco an amplitude, variety, a source of invention, continually renewed, in the treatment of customary themes.

Günther does not belong to the idyllic group; what he favored were great battles between Good and Evil, Light and Darkness, in which his unbridled imagination, which would have made him a perfect painter of battles, had free rein and mingled the fountains of mystic illumination with the unleashing of monsters and demons (the Church of Rott on the Inn, 1763). The perspective, which he breaks up and reconstructs at the dictates of his strange genius, becomes the main plastic element of a composition which often dispenses with illusionist architecture but which, when it does adopt it, gives it the value and significance of almost abstract structures.

The castles of Brühl and Bruchsal in which the rococo Baroque blossoms into its most perfect grace and dazzling splendor, owe a great deal to their respective decorators, both masters of imaginary space — Carlo Carlone and Johann Zick. Carlone (1686-1775), like Amigoni and Appiani, Italian emigrants to Germany or descendants of Italians whose service had been retained by princes, was to fall into a courtly lyricism, formal even in its exaggerations, the exuberant gesticulation of which does not always seem very sincere.

Johann Zick (1702-1759), on the other hand first comes to our notice as a small ox-drover whose gifts seem to have been the chance discovery of a journeyman painter — or so the legend would have us believe — but most of all as an artist who ended his apprenticeship at Venice whither the Austrians flocked to learn from Tiepolo's example. Zick's talent in the construction of imaginary buildings which aimed at the solidity of marble and the airiness of mist, has rarely been equalled in German Baroque painting. The virtuosity with which he merges into the suffusion of light the vast arcades and huge cupolas to which he alludes in the "White Hall" in Bruchsal (1751-1754) marks the apogee at the same time as it announces the decline of the Baroque, which has by then exhausted all its wonders.

The greatest and strangest of all this galaxy of good painters, among whom we can point to some masters of real genius, is Franz Anton Maulbertsch. At the period when Rococo was degenerating into Mannerism with Franz Anton Zeiller (1716-1774), when Thomas Huber was content with the agreeable and intriguing *chinoiseries* in which he excelled, and Johann Bergl was expending his remarkable verve and charming, though somewhat precious talent composing trompe-l'œil vistas and gardens, Maulbertsch's fiery personality constituted something truly unique. In him the Baroque temperament was teased into an alchemy of form, taken to white-heat, mixed with liquid enamels, thick and iridescent, in the crucible from which the colored matter emerged like a stream of molten lava.

Little is known of the life, training and aesthetic principles of this strange master, in whom the teaching of the Dutch is associated with striking reminiscences of Italian Baroque painters. We learn from contemporary records that he pretty rapidly acquired a considerable fame which can moreover be measured by the high sums of money he received. But this did not prevent him from leading a solitary and somewhat unhappy life, for, proud and independent, it was with a bad grace that he complied with his clients' whims. Extremely cultured, possessed of an extensive knowledge of theology, liturgy and symbolism, he built up the arrangements of his vast allegorical compositions, in which each form had a precise and exact sense, with meticulous care. This exceptionally productive artist who painted fifty-nine decorative ensembles in forty-five years which reveal an admirable variety, still found time to construct the religious compositions on the grand scale such as the decorations for the Piaristenkirche, Vienna (1750) or the great hall of Vienna University (the Theologsaal, 1756), which is informed with a rigorous and striking symbolism.

It is impossible to comprehend fully the fusion of Maulbertsch's religious philosophy and his plastic concepts without reading the detailed program he prepared for the frescoes of the church of Mühlfraun in Bohemia (1775). A professional theologian could not have done better or gone further in the choice of allegories and their symbolic disposition, the knowledge of the sacred value of colors and symbols.

We are compelled therefore to admire in Maulbertsch's works, whether sacred or profane, the depth and lucidity of the narrative and the brilliant audacity of the execution. To this must be added the fact that few painters were as much travelled as he, that Austria, Bohemia and Hungary competed for his presence in their country, that he had to satisfy the requirements of both temporal and ecclesiastical princes while continuing his teaching at the Academy of Fine Arts to which he had been appointed as professor at the age of twenty-six in 1750. Piazzetta, Ricci, Bazzani possibly contributed to his aesthetic and technical development, at all events through the medium of other people (his father, Troger), but the person to whom he owed

FRANZ ANTON MAULBERTSCH – THE VICTORY OF ST. JAMES THE GREAT OVER THE SARACENS. CIRCA 1765 (0,32; 0,48) – BAROCKMUSEUM, VIENNA

the most is Rembrandt, a large number of whose engravings, by a strange whim, he copied in oil. Maulbertsch was by temperament a great lyricist, a poet of violent impulses; he preferred working in an atmosphere of supernatural storms and almost in a state of trance. Everything in his work is movement, but the movement always comes from within, from his own zest, passion, violence, emotion His lay decorations, even, are imbued with a dramatic animation which are a far cry from Bergl's or Zimmermann's idylls. His tragic notion of human fate drives him on to destroy almost all outward forms, dissolve them in the air as if they were teased out by the drama of their movements and disintegrated in order to prove to us that we are "such stuff as dreams are made on", in the fuliginous caverns of chiaroscuro.

The verve with which he works, the fantastic freedom of his brush, impelled as it were by dynamic force, his method of modelling in the matter and color with more boldness and confidence than Rembrandt himself, are to be seen mainly in his sketches *(The Victory of St. James the Great over the Saracens,* Vienna*),* but when we examine his great decorative paintings at close quarters, we discover a truly modern treatment in touch, matter, placing of the light. If we still feel close to Spiegler's and Bergmüller's fantasies and Paul Troger's whirlwinds and the vertiginous architecture of Melchior Steidl, it is Maulbertsch who strikes us as being a "romantic" by temperament, an expressionist in practice, and when we study this climax of German Baroque decoration, we deplore more than ever the errors committed by classicism in deflecting fresco painting on the grand scale from the lyrical stream that had been its inspiration up to the end of the eighteenth century — Maulbertsch having died in 1796[16].

Too many artists obeyed the famous edict of 1777, in which the Prince Elector of Bavaria, Karl Theodor, self-appointed director of the arts, demanded 'more simplicity'. The result of this return to simplicity was a kind of desiccation, impoverishment of form and color and a failure to see the error of wanting to give reason the upper hand in an art-form that is essentially inspired by emotion and — rightly so — the irrational[17].

For some time German decorative painting on the grand scale survived the imaginationwhich had inspired it and the inexaustible inventive spirit which renewed it. It was to find a new lease of life with the kings of Bavaria and their romantic painters, By then, however, a fresh spirit prevailed. The Baroque was far distant.

PORTRAIT AND LANDSCAPE IN THE EIGHTEENTH CENTURY

TASTE for reason, progress in natural science, psychological curiosity, the importance given to inquiring and reasoning individualism that saw everything in terms of man in an anthropocentric philosophy that had dismissed God from the forefront of people's minds, gave the portrait an exceptional preponderance in this eighteenth century which, in Germany as in France, produced few religious paintings. Among these German portraitists — who were particularly prolific in the second half of the century — some still belong to the Baroque-Rococo tradition, others are steeped in classical idealism, while others again already anticipate Romanticism.

The psychological portrait, corresponding to what is in philosophy the *Aufklärung* or Age of Enlightenment, is very different from what it had been in the sixteenth century; at that time it had been the "Faustian" factor, the potential element which had counted most; now man had accepted his limitations, he no longer hankered after vast spaces; he was a definite individuality in a carefully marked-out world in which each person had his place and his function. But because this epoch was fraught with anxiety, precisely because it was one of transition, the crossroads where a dying society met one that was just born, and because each individual was devoured by an anxiety which he was too proud to reveal to the outside world, an uneasiness can be detected in the glance even of the most self-possessed. Behind this experience of dialectical knowledge of man which is the preoccupation of the analytical portraitist, we are conscious of a return to the unrevealed, the unexplored, and it is that which interests us in the works of Balthasar Denner, J.G. Edlinger, Anton Graff, principally, among whom the Baroque and Rococo characteristics are still active.

Balthasar Denner (1685-1779), a native of Hamburg, faithful to a realist tradition of the Renaissance, sought out the significant detail of the individual both in his physical and moral personality with the same patient application. He is finicky about the peculiarities of the skin, the modelling of the face; wrinkles and warts are emphasized with naturalistic fidelity, almost ingenuous in its painstakingness, as we see in *The Portrait of an Old Man* and the *Portrait of a Man in a Wig*, both in Berlin; the luxuriant beard of the former, the florid and slightly blotchy complexion of the latter have been painted according to this near-illusionist idiom. *The Portrait of an Old Man in a Fur Coat* in Dresden on the other hand is impressive in its dramatic character, the fiery glance, the tortured lips and furrowed brow. The Faustian element, already referred to, reappeared here, perhaps in spite of the artist's intentions, in a portrait in which the anxious heart is at loggerheads with the wise precepts of the reason. We meet this same phenomenon in an Austrian who had migrated to Bavaria, Johann Georg Edlinger (1741-1819), to whom something of La Tour's uneasy spirit appears to have been communicated. The group *The Bookseller Strobl and Family* (Munich) is the best example of the interest Edlinger shows in the inner life of his portrait-subjects and the way he reveals it in their faces in the somewhat mysterious light of his browns.

Edlinger has been called the "Graff of Munich"; it is, like all analogies, arbitrary and inexact. There is only one valid point of comparison between Edlinger and this Swiss from Winterthur, Anton Graff (1736-1813) — the Baroque spirit of anxiety, common to both, which, following the brief and superficial interlude of classicism, was to tie up with "romantic" anxiety. Graff is credited with the creation of the middle-class art of portraiture which proceeded independently of Baroque-Rococo aesthetics. The picturesque, not to say burlesque, picture of the *Councillor of the Consistory J.J. Spalding*, in Berlin, the amiable couple *The Martens, Man and Wife*, characteristic of the upper middle-class of Saxony in the eighteenth century, however, are of less account than his self-portraits in which he scrutinized and represented himself with a completely Rembrandtesque sincerity. As for his court portraits, they have exchanged royal finery for gracious intimacy, and correspond to the democratic temperament of this Swiss painter. He rarely took this principle as far as he did in the self-portrait which represents him sitting before his easel, turning towards the spectator with charming abandon (1786, Dresden).

Swiss likewise, but very different, the Genevan, Jean Étienne Liotard (1704-1789) never subjected his models to profound and disturbing interrogations. This amiable master, a virtuoso of the pastel, intoxicated with gay and bright colors, seduced by local color to the point that he resided in Turkey and dressed in oriental garb (he was nicknamed "the Turkish painter" because of his kaftan and his long beard in which he is swathed in his self-portrait in the museum in Geneva), belonged completely to the French slopes of Switzerland; a painter of the Austrian court and English aristocracy, this ironic, whimsical painter, rich from his noble *métier* of enamel glazing when he relinquished pastel painting, has little if any claim to be considered as belonging to German painting; setting aside his nationality, his place is rather with La Tour — one degree below — than with Graff.

The eighteenth century was the Golden Age of women painters; Rosalba Carriera in Italy, Mme Vigée Le Brun in France; Germany also had her own, Angelica Kaufmann (1741-1805) who enjoyed a fame out of all proportion to her talent

ANTON GRAFF – SELF-PORTRAIT.
1786 – (0,52; 0,41)
NATIONALGALERIE, BERLIN-DAHLEM

and the much more interesting Dorothea Therbusch (1722-1782), official painter to the King of Prussia and member of the Royal Academy of Paris. The wonderful folds of satin, the magnifying glass oddly applied to her eye in her Berlin *Self-Portrait*, bear witness to a very real talent [18].

Daniel Chodowiecki (1726-1801), a Pole with whom the Prussian Court was infatuated, is most famed for his genre painting, his "intimacies" in the spirit of Cornelis Troost — like that Dutchman, he worshipped the theatre and exploited its resources a great deal — and those paintings of groups which the English, who adored them, called "conversation pieces". Thus we are witnessing an eminently social art in which the refined simplicity of the Rococo revels in intimate receptions, at which each person follows his own bent and which corresponds at that time to the reality of court life in a great number of petty German principalities. Among these court painters we find the better of the two artists whose fame rests on his work in this genre, Johann Zoffany (1733-1810) and Januarius Zick (1732-1797). A native of Regensburg, Zoffany settled in England pretty early in his career, was appreciated by George III and painted conversation pieces which inspired inumerable imitators, for London society, which favored this mixture of intimacy and drawing room comedy. Zick had begun painting in his father's manner, and, in collaboration with him, vast monumental decorations, though by temperament he was more interested in smaller formats and genre painting. The lessons he had learned from Mengs, whose pupil he had been, inclined this son of an eminent Baroque painter towards classicism.

Despite the great number of portrait painters who competed for the favors of the courts and patrons' orders, the Tischbein tribe managed to make their way. Even more numerous than the Bach family, the Tischbeins were to be found in the majority of the great or petty courts of Germany. It would be a waste of time to name and define the known twenty-four members of this prolific line, for their merits are, like their reputations, very unequal. There is one, at any rate, whom we must mention, since he was closely connected with the life and work of Gœthe, that Wilhelm Tischbein (1751-1829) whose fame is linked up with the poet's whose companion and portraitist he was, and who is certainly responsible for having anchored in his work that uncompromising and closed classicism which made him inaccessible to the best romantic artists.

There are fewer celebrated names in landscape painting than in portraiture; it was the lesser personalities that made their names in it, and on the whole the results are disappointing. German scenery did not inspire those artists who remained indifferent to mountain lakes, pine forests such as an Everdingen, however, had already discovered in the preceding century and which animated the landscapes of the Danube School of the sixteenth century to a fantastic degree. The Romantics were to be conscious of the mysteriousness and beauty of these essentially Germanic scenes, too Germanic to be understood by the contemporaries of the *Aufklärung* with their more French culture. The German landscape painters of the eighteenth century were more familiar with nature as seen through the eyes of the Dutch, the Italians, Claude or Dughet, than the actual scenery of their own country, and spontaneously, almost involuntarily, they chose for their subject a nature that was already painted instead of painting from life. Hence the heroic pastorals of A. Faistenberger (1678-1722), Tyrolese like Koch, living in Vienna and an emulator of Salvator Rosa; the trees in the Ruisdael manner of the Bavarian painter, Josef Wagenbauer (1775-1829), and the forests of Jakob Dorner the Younger (1775-1852) whose own style is the result of copying simultaneously Everdingen, Claude Lorraine and Ruisdael; the works of the School of the Palatinate in which the Kobell family figured as often as the Ruisdaels in Holland, the former being moreover slavish imitators of the latter. Of Franz Kobell, (1749-1822) who established a curious liaison between Rococo and Romanticism, Gœthe said that he was "the first German landscape painter of his time" — which does not mean that he was a great painter. More interesting because more original and directly inspired by the oak forests of Brunswick, is Johann Friedrich Weitsch (1723-1803) whose lighting effects, sun's rays slipping through the branches of huge trees, are painted from nature with a vigorous frankness. Josef Konrad Seekatz (1719-1768), a painter of the Darmstadt Court owed his invitation to decorate the residence of the Comte de Thoranc near Grasse to the friendship and admiration of a French officer of the occupying forces. His familiarity with Fragonard's painting and the light of the Midi helped him to develop his talent, and he brought a new way of seeing things back to Germany with him.

Whether it was because they were more aware of grandiose and picturesque nature which encompassed them or whether they stuck less obstinately to foreign models, Swiss painters seem to have been in more direct contact with nature: the idyllic aspects of course, as befitted the taste of the period. Thus the most representative of them, Salomon Gessner, bucolic in his paintings as in his poems — Gessner in the eighteenth like the Austrian Adalbert Stifter in the nineteenth century — belongs to literary rather than art history, but pure painters such as J.B. Bullinger (1713-1793) and A. Ducros (1748-1810) likewise confined themselves for the most part to the idyllic aspects of nature. Pleasant exceptions to this, because they were in more direct communion with wild nature — which this epoch could hardly comprehend or even *see* — occur in the works of two painters who were in Switzerland at the same time as Koch in the Tyrol, the "revealers of the mountain", Heinrich Wüest of Zurich (1741-1821) and J.L. Aberli of Winterthur (1723-1786) who appear as precursors of a new sensibility, pre-Romantics. Around them, inspired by their examples, was grouped that rich and charming School of Swiss landscape painters who stood midway between the eighteenth and nineteenth centuries and who, in their turn, were to inspire a numerous progeny.

Landscapes, portraits, genre painting were not infrequently imbued with a new spirit which combined the Baroque-Rococo feeling, already considered rather as belonging to the past, with the anticipation of Romanticism. This new spirit was a kind of neoclassicism based on the edicts of Winckelmann in support of which Ismael Mengs (circa 1698-1764) and above all his son, Anton Raphael Mengs, much better known (1728-1779) set a practical example with a somewhat pedantic adherence to them. By imposing these two Christian names on his heir, Ismael Mengs was virtually enjoining him not to deviate from the path indicated by Raphael and Correggio. Faithful to his father's idols, Anton Raphael Mengs wrote numerous works on pictorial theory and conceived his paintings as illustrations of his teaching. When in 1839 Viardot saluted the "greatest painter of the eighteenth century" in this doctrinaire classic, it was in obedience to that extraordinary unanimity of admiration which surrounded an artist desperately anxious to reconcile the antique — as Winckelmann wanted it — with the aesthetics of the second phase of the Renaissance and to reject any element of Germanic tradition from this amalgam. He created a school likewise in Madrid where Court and Town swore by him, and wherever he trained pupils, the air was laden with an arid academism.

The mantle of neoclassicism fell on the shoulders of a painter who was even more fascinated by the antique than Mengs in Adam Friedrich Osers (1717-1799). Though much more romantic, or perhaps, *romantically classical*, Carstens' arrival on the scene is characterized by less vigor and, of course, less originality. Osers has been described, probably correctly, as the perfect representative of the "periwigged genre".

ERNST FERDINAND OEHME – CATHEDRAL IN WINTER – (1,27; 1,00) GEMÄLDEGALERIE, DRESDEN

German character had adapted itself with little success to the ideals of eighteenth century — in its classical idiom at any rate, for there is also an extremely important Romantic (or pre-Romantic) aspect. The dictates of reason had but slight effect on an art which had always depended on feeling and expression. The Romantic and Expressionist elements that already existed in the sixteenth century and the grand Baroque decoration was to receive further nutriment from this change in sensibility and conception of forms which came to the fore after the end of the eighteenth century.

If Romanticism in its essence is *the* German phenomenon, foreign contributions must not be forgotten. In Shakespeare especially, English Romanticism provided German art with a new source of inspiration, exotic enough to surprise, yet at the same time, close enough to the German temperament to be easily assimilated. Switzerland, too, with Bodner, revived ancient epics and revealed the Nibelungenlied to a people that had almost lost all memory of it. For Greek and Roman mythology, cultivated by the Classical school, was substituted that Nordic mythology mixed with Scandinavian, German and Gallic elements from which historical painters (Schnorr von Carolsfeld, Moritz von Schwind, Alfred Rethel) were to borrow subjects for their grandiose decorations. At the same time, a fresh revival of interest in the Middle Ages and Renaissance — between which they did not differentiate too clearly — inclined men's minds and sensibility towards a broader conception of medieval forms, life and thought. There was a marked tendency to re-discover the fulness of religious faith which the eighteenth century had combated but not destroyed. Medieval piety, bound up with the forms of the Gothic cathedral, picturesque and charming aspects of old-world towns that had remained unchanged since the sixteenth century (Nuremberg was "discovered") found an unexpected delight in the goodheartedness of that period, the solemnity of its buildings, the simple yet moving beauty of its works of art. In its very incompleteness, Cologne Cathedral became a symbol of German destiny; Romanticism was striving to reconstruct in its people a *medieval state of soul.* "It is we ourselves who live in the real Middle Ages, which have been falsely interpreted in previous epochs." (Schlegel).

The Boisserée brothers bought a quantity of ancient altarpieces which were about to be used as firewood, from a dealer in old junk, and formed the first collection of medieval painting. In the poetry, painting and architecture of the Middle Ages, Germany recognized the elements of a national art, something that really belonged to her. With Romanticism, Germany was conscious of herself as Germany, of her age and continuity; if she was perpetually changing, she remained ever true to herself with each metamorphosis. The castles on the Rhine, the Rhine itself with its citadels, ancient towns and cathedrals spaced along its banks, symbolize this spirit. Whereas in France the Romantic movement was somewhat artificial, in German art it represents the most profound, inalienable qualities in its basic implications, perpetually renewed and refreshed in the originality and unexpectedness of its forms. German Romanticism in one of its very important aspects is *medieval*; French Romanticism is *pseudo-medieval.*

But we must not forget however, that as in the case of the Italian Renaissance which copied Antiquity, it was the "present" in German Romanticism, the new element which proved the most fertile and interesting, not what was backward-looking. The publication of Minnesinger by Bodner (1758), chivalrous romances by Myller (1785), the *Nibelungenlied* by Bodner (1755), popular poetry by Tieck (1799), is not so much the work of historical research and scholarship as a passionate movement towards the genesis of German literature.

The return to the Middle Ages does not imply the exclusion of classical forms. Schinkel, using Hellenic idioms in his architecture, invented fantastic Gothic cathedrals in his paintings; Carstens and Fuseli were equally ready to illustrate Fingal's *Odes* or the *Odyssey.* Koch in his historical pictures divided his attention among *la Divina Commedia, Faust* and *Temora.* Wackenroder himself, medieval though he was, could proclaim that "real art did not flourish only among Corinthian columns and majestic cupolas, but also beneath ogee arches and Gothic towers." The new feeling about nature which appeared in painting and poetry in the second half of the eighteenth century in Europe and took men's eyes and sensibilities back to the forest, mountain, sea, glacier, provided an original interpretation of medieval architecture in the celebrated comparison that Schlegel made between the "forest" of Gothic columns and the monumental "aisles" which open out amidst the pine trees. The cosmic feeling for nature, man's insignificance before the vastness of the ocean or forests that stretched away as far as the eye could see, offered subjects for meditation in which Romantic sensibility was to measure by the infinity of the elements the material finiteness and spiritual infiniteness of its Faustian destiny.

Thus Romantic painting, while it amused itself with the old Germanic idyll and the re-discovery of aesthetic sources in medieval art, was to enlarge its horizon enormously in its search after pantheistic communion with free nature. But its ideal was still the union of man with the natural elements, the restoration of lost unity, the harmonious reconciliation of the individual with the universe around him.

The classicism-romanticism contradiction, which appears so false and artificial in the use commonly made of the notion, is utterly valueless when we examine the ardent classical idiom that we find in Jakob Asmus Carstens (1754-1796). This miller's son who had read Shakespeare, Homer, Dante, Ossian and Klopstock with equal zeal did not take his first lessons in painting until the age of twenty-two, at the Academy of Fine Art in Copenhagen. His knowledge of Michelangelo, Guido Reni, Raphael and Correggio was derived from the engravings he had seen of their work; the sculptors he knew through plaster casts which, he confessed, inspired in him a feeling of sacred veneration, deep enough for tears. He worked alone, without a model, drawing impressive imaginative scenes suggested by his favorite books. Intuitively he discovered the truly classical and did not fall for academicism in the Mengs manner. He had no desire to copy the antique; he made it live through the power of his personal sense of the tragedy of life and the strength of his drawing. He seldom took his paintings beyond the cartoon stage, but for him the cartoon was an end in itself and his work appears as a kind of synthesis of plastic monumentality and inward emotion. *The Birth of Light* and *Light and her Brood* (Weimar) are the best examples of this grandiose dynamism.

The manner Carstens had of treating classical themes romantically is equally to be found — though with a marked predilection for Hellenism — in that curious artist Bonaventura Gemelli (1798-1863). He had been the personal friend of the Nazarenes and he even lived for some time in their group. His imagination is less febrile and fantastic than Carstens'; his art not so tragic, although it has a distinct leaning towards Baroque rhetoric. But in him the inward life is not so emphatic or authentic. It is true that he adopted some of the pseudo-medieval themes — the life of a witch, the life of an artist — but he preferred subjects drawn from the fable or mythology. His ideal of beauty brings him close to the kind of romantic classicism which, before such terms were invented, had been that of the School of Fontainebleau whose aesthetic principles of the small graceful heads set on powerful bodies he had adopted.

Whether we are dealing with William Blake or Carstens we find the strange personality of Hans Heinrich Füssli (Henry Fuseli, 1741-1825) behind this eclectic tendency. Lavater said of him, "his glance is lightning, his word the storm," and he himself, evoking his own work, made the following tragic confession, "I advance in a sea that has neither shore nor bottom," A great reader, occasionally writing poetry, he was the first artist to illustrate the *Nibelungen* which had been revealed to him by his spiritual father, Bodmer. Fuseli, however, transformed the ancient German heroes into characters from the *Iliad*. He had learned a great deal from Joshua Reynolds in England, Michelangelo in Italy, and he worshipped Rubens. For him, as for the majority of the Romantics, Shakespeare was a god and he never tired of illustrating *The Midsummer Night's Dream*. His best works are those in which

HENRY FUSELI – THE LITTLE FAIRY. CIRCA 1795 – (0,635; 0,765) KUNSTMUSEUM, BASLE

against a red and tawny chiaroscuro he conjures up fantastic figures — the horse of *The Nightmare* (Zurich), the *Little Fairy* of Basle, the gigantic heroes of Ariosto and Milton. He allows the supernatural to appear on the surface of lifelike figures with the ingenuous candor of a clairvoyant, which enables him to move effortlessly in the unreal world which was his true reality.

Joseph Anton Koch and Peter von Cornelius were familiar with his work. The former's *Witches of Macbeth*, the latter's *Death of Kriemhild* (1811) could not have been what they were without Fuseli and Carstens. The same is true of the *Entombment* (1806) of Eberhard Wächter (1762-1852), or *Macbeth with the Weird Sisters* by Franz Pforr (1808).

The reproach brought against Romantic painting of being "literary" is directed at them because it is in point of fact a kind of painting in which the subject counts a great deal, and the aesthetic problems are not the only ones confronted. It requires however no effort on our part to recognize that despite this frequent attachment to the anecdote, the latter is never more than a point of departure, a stimulus to creation, around which the emotion radiates and expands. The profusion and variety of outstanding personalities in Romantic art is the best evidence of this.

RELIGIOUS PAINTING

THE great German religious art which had blossomed forth in the sumptuous splendor of Baroque, branches off with the Romantic movement towards an aesthetic principle inspired by the German Middle Ages and the first phase of the Italian Renaissance. The imitation element is preponderant and yet we have no reason to doubt the artists' sincerity. When the Nazarenes set up in the Roman abbey of Sant' Isidoro, living a semi-monastic existence and considering art as an act of worship for which they prepared themselves by prayer, following the wish expressed by Cornelius, they were not merely yielding to an artificial fashion; they were obeying a profound aspiration, and it was that, perhaps, that gave their works the medieval simplicity which seems affected to us, even literary, but for them it was not so.

The Nazarene movement, however, did not start up in an ancient German town but in Vienna, the cosmopolitan, the eclectic, and it was in Italy that it came to fruition, even if its doctrine was based on Wackenroder's *Effusions of an Artist-Monk*. It was in Vienna that Johann Friedrich Overbeck (1789-1869) struck up a friendship with Eberhard Wächter who had brought with him Carstens' classico-modern ideal and studied copies of Italian frescoes of the fifteenth and sixteenth centuries, made by Franz Riepenheusen (1786-1831). His intimacy with the ardent and generous Franz Pforr (1788-1812) who was destined to die at the age of twenty-four and who, as we shall see, was one of the most original and attractive masters of this at once ancient and modern religious aestheticism, led him to found the *Lukas-bund* (Brotherhood of St. Luke) in 1809 and, the following year, to set up in Rome where he was converted to Catholicism in 1813. The Abbey of Sant' Isidoro became a rallying point. The Italian atmosphere, contact with the Old Masters, reading of Dante, most of all, the cult of Raphael—for the Nazarenes passed over the Primitives—developed an aesthetic system not so much archaic in approach as classical, since their models were, above all, the painters of the Classical Renaissance, as the fresco cycles of the Casa Bartholdy and Villa Massimi—commissions made possible by the favor and support of the German consul and a great Italian noble—prove to us. Friedrich Overbeck died at the age of eighty in the Rome which he had not left for more than half a century, except in 1831, to pay a short visit to the Rhineland.

Overbeck intended to follow what he called the 'three ways of art'—that of imagination represented by Michelangelo, that of beauty represented by Raphael, and that of nature represented by Dürer. Wintergest, Vogel, Hottinger, Sutter were among the first members of the Brotherhood: they are the least known, however, in that considerable team of Romantic artists who revived religious painting. Their works have been largely neglected whereas we now do justice to the real originality and indisputable importance of Carl Philipp Fohr (1795-1818), Scheffer von Leonards-hoff (1796-1822), Heinrich Maria Hess (1798-1863), Passavant, Ramboux, Schnorr von Carolsfeld, Wilhelm Schadow (1786-1862), the brothers Olivier, Joseph von Führich (1800-1876) and Joseph Anton Koch (1768-1839) who was also, as we shall see, the creator of the Romantic landscape.

One of the most remarkable and attractive figures of the religious art of this period is Maria Alberti, daughter of a Hamburg protestant pastor and converted to Catholicism, and who, after a visit to a gallery at Dresden, became enamored of Italian Renaissance art. She looked after Novalis up to the time of his death and died herself in 1812 while engaged in nursing the typhus victims in the nunnery of the Sisters of Mercy of Münster in Westphalia, where she had taken the veil four years previously and where the majority of her extremely rare works are kept. In her generous personality, in her everyday life perhaps even more than in her art, Maria Alberti is a magnificent representative of the Romantic artist.

Side by side with Overbeck whose drawings and portraits have more vigor than his pious compositions—the best of which is probably *Joseph sold into captivity* (1816), though it remains cold and artificial in its "Raphaelism"—we must place the other eminent personality, at least as far as inspiration is concerned—of the Nazarene movement, Peter von Cornelius (1783-1867). Their aesthetic principles can be compared by studying the episode of the *Life of Joseph*, painted at this same period by Cornelius, in the Casa Bertholdy previously mentioned which is now also in the Nationalgalerie, Berlin. Whereas Overbeck shows a Perugino tendency, Cornelius seems more attracted by Michelangelo. He signed his childhood letters with the name Raphael, dreamed of Italy of whose pagan antiquities and Christian art he was equally enamored, and his mother had formed the habit of walking him up and down at night in the Gallery of Antiquities in the Dresden Museum, of which his father was the Keeper, to soothe his childish insomnia. He was trained later in Vienna among the Titians and Correggios but he went back to old German art when, in 1808, he was infatuated with the Book of Hours of the Emperor Maximilian, to which Dürer and his great contemporaries had contributed. The illustrations for *Faust* reveal an energetic return to the German spirit, and through his relationship with Sulpiz Boisserée he was initiated into the marvelous world of ancient German painting. In the Nazarene circle of Sant' Isidoro, in love with a beautiful Roman woman whom he was to marry and under the domination of Overbeck, Cornelius was to remain in Italy and execute fresco painting in the spirit of the Florentine Renaissance, until his final return to Germany.

In his Roman frescoes, as in those he did for the Ludwigskirche in Munich (1836-1839) and his projects for the Campo Santo of Berlin, never carried out but which occupied him the latter part of his life, Cornelius remained under the spell of this aesthetic system that had its roots in the past.

If Overbeck and Cornelius can be described, without mincing matters, as "Italianizing," other Romantic painters, less famous but, in my opinion, greater, owed a debt to the Middle Ages and the German Renaissance for their archaic innovation—paradoxical though the juxtaposition of these words may seem,—comparable to what Tieck, Brentano, Arnim, and the *Heinrich von Ofterdingen* of Novalis did in the domain of poetry during the same period. This is particularly true of Johann Anton Ramboux (1790-1866) who retained a certain Teutonic candor and medieval ingenuousness, Ludwig Sigismund Ruhl (1794-1887), who favored the troubadour genre *(The Fair Melusina at her Toilet,* Mannheim), Johann David Passavant (1787-1861) who after working with David and Baron Gros in Paris, joined the *Lukasbund* and lived in Rome.

The case of Schnorr von Carolsfeld (1794-1872) and Carl Philipp Fohr (1795-1818) is quite different. The former divided his attention, as as far as subjects are concerned, between the *Nibelungenlied* (1832-1845) and Ariosto (1820-1826). His religious painting combines a certain Italian gentleness with the sharper notes of fifteenth and sixteenth century Franconian realism. Obviously inspired by Dürer in the matter of the facial expressions of his personages, he idealizes and at the same time remains true to an almost naturalistic objectivity. Fohr, who was accidentally drowned in the Tiber at the age of twenty-three, was, with Pforr, one of the really promising geniuses of the new school. He was one of the finest creators of the lyrical landscape which starts with Koch and ends with Friedrich, Carus and Oehme. His vigorous talent, which renders all his portraits almost the equal of those of the Old German Masters, the attentive study of their technique, bring him close to Altdorfer and Cranach, especially in his *Return from the Hunt* (Schlossmuseum, Darmstadt) which we can compare with sixteenth century compositions; whilst his *Murgthal Chapel* is imbued with the freshest Romantic as well as medieval sensibility.

Franz Pforr, who died at Albano at the age of twenty-four, was one of the very first to join the *Lukasbund* movement, in 1809; he set up in Rome in company with Overbeck, Vogel, Wintergest and other "brothers" and, like them, he became enthusiastic about Italian art. His premature death allowed him an all-too-brief stay in Rome and Naples. In Pforr there was still a great deal of that ingenuous sensibility which we associate with the Old German Masters; from some points of view in the feeling and even the manner of painting, he seems almost a Primitive. I mean particularly in compositions such as *The Entry of Rudolph von Hapsburg into Basle* (1809-1810, Frankfort), or *Graf von Hapsburg and the Priest* (1809), which are treated entirely in the spirit of the sixteenth century; he was free of any preconceived archaic ideas, and this merely because his character, his feeling for ancient tradition, his freshness of spirit and his desire to imitate no one, especially not the Masters to whom the other Nazarenes felt most attracted, preserved him from slavish adherence to the notion of ideal beauty and "Gothic classicism."

Moving in a similar direction to that taken by Pforr were the brothers Olivier (Ferdinand, 1785-1841) and Heinrich (1783-1848) who, with the third brother Friedrich (1791-1859), played an important rôle in the building-up and evolution of the Romantic landscape. It is above all the landscape that distinguishes *Christ's Baptism* which Ferdinand and Heinrich painted in collaboration between 1808 and 1810 (Wörlitz). The Jordan Valley as here represented could have been painted by an artist of the Danube School, and the bands of angels and spectators are treated with imagination and picturesqueness, characteristic of the Germans of the Renaissance. The sincere faith, taste for the marvelous, acceptance of the supernatural also find their true expression in the *Vision of St. Hubert,* linked with a forceful realism—rare qualities, but combined again in the two most exquisite interpreters of the resuscitated and legendary Middle Ages, Moritz von Schwind and Ludwig

Richter; whereas Alfred Rethel (1816-1859), more distinguished as a draughtsman and engraver than as a painter, under the influence of the events of the 1848 Revolution re-discovered in his famous *Totentanz* the demoniac humor of the ancient *danses macabres*.

The best of Rethel occurs in the furious battles of the Nibelungen and knight-errants, the funereal and mocking apparitions of disguised skeletons. He went mad at the age of thirty and plunged into a world of hallucinations and ghosts which had already begun to haunt him even when in full possession of his reason.

Local color, fidelity to details of period and country, rejection of classical conventions, endowed the works of the Romantic painters of historical subjects with an originality and freshness which still remains the attraction of those vast compositions, long cycles of mural decorations, derived from the events of the Middle Ages or ancient Greek legend, such as those painted by Alfred Rethel at Aix-la-Chapelle. The frescoes of Schnorr von Carolsfeld and Moritz von Schwind, whose vehemence is sincere even in its grandiloquence, have already been mentioned. Among the minor artists who lacked neither inspiration nor talent we should include two of Pforr's pupils who were also the restorers of the medieval panels of the Boisserée Collection, namely Wintergest and Xeller.

These works, which the collectors found at the second-hand dealers or firewood-merchants, were in a shocking state, and to restore them the Romantic painters who piously undertook this task first initiated themselves in the technique of the old masters. Wintergest and Xeller refined and clarified their art in the process of restoring these works. Similarly, Ferdinand Hartmann (1774-1842) and Ferdinand August Fellner (1799-1859) acclimatized their gift of invention and originality to the sixteenth century manner; a specialist in medieval costume, Fellner clothed the characters of the *Nibelungenlied*, to which he devoted a suite of engravings, in a less whimsical way than Cornelius, while remaining true to this Gothic-Romantic spirit which was not yet that of the troubadour genre, though it anticipated it, and was regarded at that time as local color.

The Romantics, in point of fact, were neither antiquarians, archeologists nor archivists. They were devoted to the past centuries with the kind of nostalgia one has for a Golden Age of beauty and harmony. Thus they made an effort to revive the Middle Ages, not exactly as it had been in the past but as they imagined it was in their own time.

THE PAINTERS OF NOSTALGIA

Nostalgia for whatever is remote in time and space, for those things to which "distance lends enchantment" and adorns with illusory magic, for old Germany with its chivalry and piety, its attractive "picturesqueness" and good-natured simplicity, for Italy with its warm landscape, free gaiety, that *Sehnsucht* which is one of the basic elements in German character, came into its own in the Romantic period more than at any other time; and it was among the second generation of Romantic artists, most strongly influenced by the poets who fed on this nostalgia for the past, Tieck, Eichendorff, Mörike, Brentano, Arnim, even Novalis and Kleist that this escape into the past was still more emphasized. Late Romanticism if you will, which is merely the prolongation of the heroic period of the precursors, (Richter, Steinle, Spitzweg died after 1880, at the time when naturalism was enjoying its triumph in Germany, thus connecting up with the Post-Romanticism of Welti, Böcklin, Feuerbach and Hodler), but Romanticism nevertheless and in the strongest sense of the term. For these victims of nostalgia, painting was like poetry, the means of recreating and resuscitating the past. They were essentially poets, painter-poets whose art is narrative and descriptive and therefore capable of rivalling the poets in their gift of evoking and materializing the very substance of dreams. Their common ground in taste and aspiration with the writers caused them to become illustrators to such an extent that their great decorative cycles are often illustrations enlarged to monumental dimensions (the historic and legendary frescoes of Moritz von Schwind at Hohenschwangau, at the Wartburg, 1854, at the Residenz at Munich, 1832) and their pictures sometimes look like a mere commentary on a text familiar to everybody, derived from epics, legends and fabliaux.

The most famous of these artists who devoted themselves to the happy yet at the same time melancholy evocation of the glorious and charming past, Moritz von Schwind (1804-1871), was like Steinle a Viennese. He had begun his career in the entourage of Cornelius and the brothers Olivier, but temperamentally he had little inclination to follow in the wake of the Nazarenes. Although he made a successful start with his vast decorations and historical subjects, his favorite subjects were the familiar legends of Melisande or the Seven Ravens, the songs of Roland's Horn, familiar or family scenes of the merchant class or feudal life in Germany in the "olden" days. What he described with all the effusiveness of his heart and exuberance of his imagination, were romantic love stories and variations on the theme he called the *Honeymoon*, the genesis and blossoming of a passion in the *Symphony* (Münich), the attractive romances of chivalry *(The Cavalcade of Kuno von Falkenstein*, Leipzig), the world of magicians and fairies *(The Dance of the Elves*, Münich, 1844). The real and fabulous occur simultaneously in his work quite naturally and without any feeling of surprise. A delightful yet accurate interpreter of the Vienna and Bavaria of his time, likewise a poet of the idealized Middle Ages, Moritz von Schwind, exuberant, productive, facile, reflects the very image of grace and happiness.

His world is the same as that of his compatriot, Eduard Jakob von Steinle (1810-1886) who was also affected by the influence of Overbeck, Führich and Cornelius with whom he lived in Rome for five years. His imagination exactly reflects the atmosphere of those marvelous German fairy tales full of symbolism whose naivety and mystery he leaves intact. His Middle Ages is that of the idyllic adventures of travelling scholars and exploits of knight-errants. The nostalgic painters of the second Romantic generation carve out a Middle Ages in conformity with their aspirations and desires, indifferent as to whether the image that they give corresponds to reality or not. What they express in this way is a Middle Ages of their own, one of dreams and imagination, very different from that which their immediate predecessors wanted to create. The gabled houses and cathedral spires which rise in the background of Steinle's picture *Extract from the Chronicle of a Traveling Scholar*, reconstruct a setting which speaks to the sensibility and the imagination.

Adrian Ludwig Richter (1803-1884) whose name and fame has been popularized by numerous illustrated books to the extent of making us forget that he was also a great painter, likewise had his Roman period between 1823 and 1828. Back in his native Saxony, he worked in the Meissen porcelain factory, which explains the detailed and almost miniaturist element in some of his works. He, too, lived in the magic world of myth which he described in poetic, musical, extremely moving accents, as in *Genevieve of Brabant* of the Kunsthalle, Hamburg (1841), which with *In a Boat on the Danube* (Dresden) is his most characteristic work. A poet of the forest, childhood, of ingenuous and fantastic tales, old houses with dovecotes slumbering beneath the snow, Richter reveals more humor than melancholy in his form of nostalgia.

The painter and engraver, Ludwig von Maydell (1795-1846), a prolific illustrator, author of numerous religious paintings, to which we may be forgiven for pre-

LUDWIG RICHTER – MOUNTAIN LAKE. 1839 – (0,63; 0,88) NATIONALGALERIE, BERLIN-DAHLEM

MORITZ VON SCHWIND – THE EMPEROR MAXIMILIAN ON THE MARTINSWAND, CIRCA 1860 – (0,59; 0,42) BAROCKMUSEUM, VIENNA

ferring his books, worked in the same idiom. Like William Blake he combined calligraphy and illuminating almost in the same spirit as Eugen Napoleon Neurenther (1806-1882), for whom the newly invented medium of lithography, so suited to the Romantic temperament, provided the means of expression which exactly corresponded to his outlook.

The fame of Karl Spitzweg (1806-1885) as an illustrator, the humor and drollery of his small pictures, his penchant for the comical, have long relegated this "little master" to the category of minor artists, and it is only recently that the charm of his color, his paint, which is as warm as that of the Old Dutch Masters with whom this Bavarian has much affinity, has been remarked. Thus, we overlooked the poetic harmony of those shady landscapes such as his truly Ruisdaelian *Idyll in the Forest.* As opposed to his contemporaries, he does not appear to have spent any time in Italy, and the behavior of the "Romanists" does not appear to have affected him. It would be interesting on the other hand to assess what influence France, in which he travelled, had on his work. What we know best are his genre paintings. He is the recorder of life's little ironies, small medievalized townships, rather like theater décor and which you only needed to copy, not very long ago either, to recapture the atmosphere of the Mastersingers. The narrator and his stories sometimes cause us to forget the painter, which is a pity. And it was probably the weakness of these "painters of nostalgia" in an art founded on the "subject" that they drew the spectator's attention solely to the contents and thus led him to neglect and overlook the truly artistic merits of the picture which were far from negligible. Targets of the horror of "anecdotal painting" reserved for conventional and academic painters, the Romantics have suffered from this denial of justice, this systematic disparagement of everything that is not pure painting. In their assocation of art, poetry and music, the three Romantic arts gained much more than they lost in this communion.

THE LANDSCAPE

MAN, "contemplating the magnificent unity of a natural landscape, takes stock of his own insignificance, and, feeling that everything is in God, loses himself in this infinity, and to some extent renounces his own individual existence. To be engulfed in this way is not to lose oneself; it is a gain; what normally you can perceive only through the intellect becomes accessible almost to the physical eye which becomes convinced about the unity of the infinite universe."

These lines extracted from *Nine Letters on Landscape-painting* by Carl Gustav Carus, sum up the new feeling which artists took as their guide. Taken as a whole and despite the tremendous variety of temperaments and talents, the Romantic landscape can be distinguished fundamentally from all other great periods of landscape painting in European art—for example the Impressionist School, the Dutch masters of the seventeenth century—and more nearly approaches Chinese landscape painting of the Sung dynasty in that it abounds in emotion that is both magic and mysterious and eminently religious. It is not a portion of the exterior aspects of nature that the painter transfers to his canvas but a veritable physical and spiritual communion with nature.

Joseph Anton Koch (1768-1839), seems, from this point of view, to be the creator of the Romantic landscape, although also a religious painter with a more or less direct allegiance to the Nazarenes; what counts most in his pictures is not the pious anecdote but the setting in which it occurs. This Tyrolese of Elgiblenalp, who settled in Rome when he had barely attained his thirtieth year and lived there up to his death, forty-five years later, worked in the atmosphere of the Campagna and in a spirit not far removed from that of Claude and Poussin. The new and effective element in his landscape painting, especially when he describes the sites of his native country or the Bernese Oberland—the *Bernese Landscape* of Innsbruck Museum (1817), or the *Schmagdribachfall*—is above all in the poetic composition which builds up the picture like a poem, each part of the canvas being a kind of descriptive stanza. This narrative conception rests on a basis of absolute realism, in the sense that Koch is one of the first to have known how to understand and express mountains, discover the beauty which lies hidden beneath their wildness, commune with elements that his contemporaries almost unanimously judged frightening and terrible.

When we examine his religious pictures, we note that the figures could be effaced from the canvas without any sense of loss; the life of the elements, the power of water forcing its way past the rocks, the majesty of the Tyrolese forest, the sunny harmony of the Roman hills, animated with a handful of factories, constitute the real subject. We might hold it against Koch that he added such anecdotal elements to the landscape with which they fail to harmonize, but this is precisely because his enjoyment of nature and his transcription in the created work are his dominant preoccupations[19].

Famous for the revival he brought about of Greek forms and their introduction into German architecture, a passionate partisan of classicism in the antique mode, Karl Friedrich Schinkel is chiefly known and admired for the new aspect he gave Berlin between 1816 and 1824. It is not so generally known—though it is the most interesting and admirable part of his work—that he was also a Romantic painter, worshipped Gothic art and that his best pictures are those in which a medieval cathedral, almost as fantastic as Gustave Doré's, dominates a dramatic landscape of rivers and woods. Schinkel (1781-1841) thus presents a dual personality, one of the richest and most curious of that period, making him almost simultaneously a man of antiquity and a man of the Middle Ages. To gain a better understanding of this complex artist, we must remember that Schinkel was for a considerable time a "man of the theater," a stage designer, and that in this capacity he found himself called upon to dress *The Magic Flute* in the antique style and the dramas of the *Sturm und Drang* within the full panoply of Romanticism. There may be a theatrical side to his Gothic cathedral which soars aloft in the midst of his forests in the illumination of an apotheosis, but it interferes neither with the sincerity of his passionate inspiration nor the validity of the semi-real, semi-dream Middle Ages which he describes.

It is Schinkel who, at a time when the young painter, Carl Blechen (1798-1840) was kicking his heels in Berlin, obtained for him the post of decorator of the theater of Königstadt, after which he set off for Italy. Of a somber cast of mind and inclined to the fantastic, Blechen, who was to die demented at the age of forty-two, left some quite good Roman landscapes, but his essential contribution consists of those striking imaginary compositions such as *The Thunderbolt*, mountain scenes and tragic and awe-inspiring forests and ruined churches in deserted valleys: *A Glen in Winter* (Berlin, 1825); *Ruined Chapel* (Königsberg, 1835). It is difficult for us at the present time to form any idea of the tormented and tragic genius of this painter, for his finest works disappeared in the conflagration which in 1931 destroyed a considerable part of the Exhibition of Romantic Painting in the Glaspalast in Munich; and what is true for Blechen is also true for many great Romantics, Carus, Runge, Friedrich, for example.

KARL BLECHEN – CAVE ON THE GULF OF NAPLES. 1829 – (0,372; 0,285) WALLRAF-RICHARTZ-MUSEUM, COLOGNE

In Blechen, as in Schinkel, we recognize the theatricality already mentioned, and also a powerful musical atmosphere reminiscent of an opera or a symphony. The stage-sets which Blechen painted for Weber's *Freischütz* have remained one of the outstanding examples of the adaptation of the Romantic idiom to the theater.

It has been said of Caspar David Friedrich (1774-1840) that "he had discovered the tragedy in landscape"; the observation emanated from David d'Angers who visited him at Greifswald, that foggy North Sea township where he lived the greater part of his life and whose landscape, which he so often painted, affected him more than anything else. Although he enjoyed his life as a recluse, Friedrich's influence on the Romantic landscape was incalculable—especially on Ferdinand von Olivier (1785-1841), Goerg Friedrich Kersting (1785-1847), Gerhard von Kügelgen, Ferdinand Hartmann (1774-1842), the Riepenhausen brothers and the strange Ernst Ferdinand Oehme (1797-1855) whose best works might have been painted by the master rather than the disciple.

Passionate in his study and contemplation of reality, Friedrich drew trees and flowers in great detail, analyzed cloud forms at great length, scrutinized the mystery of rocks and metals; but his visionary genius then seized hold of such data and transformed them, unmasking, as it were, their hidden life. His art consists of self-examination, contemplation, meditation, deep study of the emotions of man in his union with Panic forces and soul of the universe. "The only true source of art," he said, "is the heart, the language of the pure and innocent soul. A picture which does not have its genesis in that can only be vain sleight of hand. Any genuine work is conceived in a sacred moment, born in a blessed hour—an impulse from within often created it, unbeknown to the artist himself." He also loved vast spaces in which the glance and imagination could be lost, prolonged and re-discovered. He interpreted the sacred majesty of the mountains, the infinity of the sea, the magic sweep of the rainbow over the rain clouds with more power than any other artist. One day he showed Cornelius a study of reeds and said, "God is everywhere, even in a grain of sand. Here I have revealed him in the reeds." The ruins of great Gothic abbeys which he often chose for his subject spoke to him of the precarious nature of all things, of death which destroys human beings and buildings alike.

Boundless space, as it were, absorbed him, whether it was a question of the *Cliffs of Rügen* of the Reinhart collection, or of waves over which great sailing boats move, or of mountain views extending as far as the eye can see. But even in the most empty landscapes in which land and sea are reduced to a thin strip, leaving all the room for the sky, there is always a tiny figure, making a stain of color around which the chromatic construction of the composition is organized—the man walking in the *Mountain Landscape with Rainbow* of the Folkwang Museum, Essen, the diminutive figure in the *Monk by the Seashore* of Berlin. In the *Two Men Contemplating the Moon* of Dresden (1819), the rapt attention of the characters underlines the mysterious phosphorescence of the globe, half-masked by clouds and branches.

You must learn by experiencing, become the thing in order to get to know the soul and even the underlying form of nature. "Close your physical eye," he said, "so that you may look first at your picture with the spiritual eye, then bring to the light of day what you have seen in the darkness. In that way the image may act on whoever looks at it from the outside towards the inside." Friedrich did not suffer

CASPAR DAVID FRIEDRICH – MONK BY THE SEASHORE. 1808 – (1,10; 1,71) NATIONALGALERIE, BERLIN-DAHLEM

from nostalgia for the Middle Ages, since he lived at the very heart of things, in the stream of elemental forces, far away from all literary inspiration. In the paintings in which he associated forest, mountain and the cross (or church)—the *Cross in the Riesengebirge* (Berlin), the *Cross of Teschen* (1806, Berlin)—he aimed at expressing that universal religion, which he adopted, in which the elements celebrate the splendors and mysteries of divinity.

No one is more Romantic than he, in the fullest sense of that term, in his intimate relationship with the supernatural, in the interior and exterior harmony between man and nature, splendor and simplicity, that such a qualification implies. Everything in his pictures expresses power, everything lives: space in itself is a value, but in a very different way than in the Old Dutch Masters, for space here is the very presence of the sacred, it is an emanation from the divine. No artist was more modest, more indifferent to the judgment of his contemporaries and to success. During his last years he was out of his mind; like Schumann in music and Hölderlin in poetry, he had advanced too far in his endeavor to fix and express the inexpressible.

Carl Gustav Carus (1789-1869), doctor, professor of gynecology in Dresden, botanist, *Natur-philosoph*, writer, was at the same time one of the most representative painters of German Romanticism and the principal theorist of the landscape doctrine. As a painter he was self-taught, and Friedrich's work revealed to him that Panic and mysterious conception of nature which he was to build up into a system in his books, *Nine Letters on Landscape Painting* (Leipzig, 1831), *Twelve Letters on the Life of the Earth* (1841), and a voluminous collection of memoirs and aphorisms. A powerful poetic feeling led him to express this mingling of the individual and the elements in his pictures, this way of "becoming things," identifying yourself with what you see, finding the divine and spiritual in the most humble objects. Carus *felt* the secret life of rocks, fogs, dormant waters, mist-clothed mountains with a fantastic intensity. The *King of the Alders*, the *Moonlight on the Reeds* and the *Walker in a Rocky Landscape during the night*, destroyed by the conflagration of 1931, *The Graveyard at Oybin* (Leipzig), express the patience with which his inner eye scrutinized the mystery of nature.

CASPAR DAVID FRIEDRICH – CONTEMPLATING THE MOON. 1819 – (0,35; 0,44) GEMÄLDEGALERIE, DRESDEN

KARL GUSTAV CARUS – THE GRAVEYARD AT OYBIN. 1828 – (0,675; 0,52) MUSEUM, LEIPZIG

Thanks to this faculty for penetrating the forms of material substance, Carus escaped the limitations of the theorist. However much interest we have in his books, without an acquaintance with which we cannot wholly comprehend the Romantic movement, it is his paintings we need to study in order to understand this curious artistic temperament[20].

PHILIPP OTTO RUNGE

THE total union of nature and the artist in the work of Philipp Otto Runge (1777-1810) offers all the characteristics of an intimate fusion of the soul, intellect and senses. Destined for commerce, he frequented first the artistic circles of Hamburg, then of Copenhagen; he came under the influence of Carstens and Friedrich, and thanks to the devotion of his brother Daniel, who promised to back him up in his needs, plunged into his career as a painter. It was to his brother Daniel that he wrote the letters in which we find this exaltation of nature-worship, this pantheistic emotion in the presence of moonlight and sunsets, during which he felt the infinite

PHILIPP OTTO RUNGE – AMARYLIS FORMOSISSIMA. 1808 – (0,56; 0,32) KUNSTHALLE, HAMBURG

breath of God. He dreamed too of discovering what a poet like Novalis and a naturalist philosopher like Schubert called "the key of life." He saw the whole universe constructed according to a system of secret correspondences between the seasons, hours of the day, ages of man, colors, forms, flowers, stars; to know and represent these was to restore to the world that unity which rationalism had loosened by disassociating matter from intelligence. Runge's all-important work was to be that monumental series (unhappily unfinished) of his *Hours of the Day*, represented by people, plants, stars, constituting a totality in the sense that the contemplation of these paintings, placed in an edifice especially constructed for that purpose, was to be accompanied by music and singing. His premature death at the age of thirty-three reduced this vast project to a series of sketches which give, however, a fair idea of what his aims were. He regarded these compositions, of which only sketches remain, as "spiritual landscapes," constructed according to the principles of the perfection of forms and proportions, of which flowers provide an example. The symbolism of colors was added to that of forms and numbers. "The light is the sun," he wrote, "which we cannot look at; but as it descends to the earth and mankind, the sky reddens. Blue awakens in us a certain veneration; it is the Father, and red is usually the intermediary between the heavens and the earth; when they both disappear, then, during the night, comes fire which is yellow and the consoler which has been sent to us; the moon too is yellow."

Runge's drawing, which has a classical purity relating it to William Blake's, was practiced with the most minute detail in his plant and flower studies; he also kept a certain angelic or childlike innocence in his nudes. Runge was fond of painting for children because childhood was for him, as for Novalis, the Golden Age. His mystic dreaminess was responsible for his failure ever to complete what he undertook, since the realization could never come up to his imagination. Nevertheless Runge would not have been the great artist he was, at the apex of German Romanticism, if all these contrasts, ambitions, aspirations towards the absolute and infinite had not been present in his heart.

THE PORTRAIT

THIS yearning to merge oneself into nature, to become one with the universe around, explains why portraiture was less important for the Romantic than for the man of the eighteenth century. Psychological curiosity dictated by intelligence played a smaller rôle than the tragic feeling of life. As in the sixteenth century, the human face expressed the drama of "being" and "becoming", anxiety, passion, the tragic scrutiny. It is this quality that appears, above all, in these prototypes such as the self portraits by Caspar David Friedrich, the *Adolescent* of the Print Room in Copenhagen, the *Mature man approaching madness* in the Nationalgalerie, Berlin. We can find a strange analogy between these portraits and landscapes by Friedrich, both being equally exciting, tormented from within by a kind of subterranean anxiety, modeled from without by the elements.

Philipp Otto Runge's portraits are more tranquil since the artist lived in a state of peace and close communion with nature. The drawing that he made to Goethe's order in 1805 (Goethe Nationalmuseum, Weimar) is a work that is profound yet uncomplicated and still more revealing than the *Self Portrait in a Blue Coat*, of the same year (Kunsthalle, Hamburg) which would be almost superficial if the glance did not possess a kind of dominating presence. The most handsome of these self portraits is that of *The man in a Brown Coat*, one of the latest works, since it is dated 1810. In this picture as in Friedrich's, the mountainous side of the face in its bold, rough modelling suggests that the man himself was a microcosm, comparable to the earth itself which Leonardo da Vinci compared to a living being.

Among the Romantic portraits representative both of this effusive emotion and the tendency to treat the human face as a piece of landscape, we ought to mention that of *Schopenhauer* by Ludwig Sigismond Ruhl; the *Portrait of the Painter Julius Oldach*, by Erwin Speckter, who was a friend of Overbeck and Cornelius (Private Collection, Munich), very interesting for the way this pencil sketch, heightened with white, recalls the drawings of Baldung, Dürer or Cranach. A *Portrait of an Old Woman* (Berlin) in the same spirit and the same technique, by Overbeck, testifies to what extent these Germano-Romans of Sant'Isidoro, these Italianizers, followed the tradition of their Renaissance predecessors, and it is probable that when Victor Emil Janssen (Hamburg) painted his self-portrait, naked to the waist, in front of his easel, he had in mind Dürer's drawing, of roughly the same pose, which he sent to his doctor whom he was consulting about his liver complaint.[21]

The comparative rarity of the portrait in the Romantic period is characteristic of an age that subordinated the individual to outside nature. We notice too that in a great number of pictures at this time, the subject of the portrait is represented with his back half-turned towards the spectator and with his gaze fixed on something beyond, in the distance, which the latter can hardly see, if indeed he can see it at all: Carus' *Boating on the Elbe* (Düsseldorf) for example, Moritz von Schwind's *Morning* (Vienna), Friedrich's *Woman at the Window* (Berlin). The poses are significant of the state of mind of an artist who is searching for an escape into space, the least attention being accorded the human face of the person who is eluding the spectator; we find the same thing often enough in the work of that Romantic painter before his time, Antoine Watteau.

ARNOLD BÖCKLIN – THE HONEYMOON. 1875 – (0,65; 0,51)
GOTTFRIED KELLER FOUNDATION, BERNE

It is told of Böcklin that one day when he was looking at Wilhelm Leibl's celebrated realist painting, *Three Women in Church*, he pointed to the peasant girl's shawl and remarked, "Leibl has painted it as painstakingly as possible. It really looks embroidered. If Leibl had actually embroidered it he could not have taken more time than he did to paint it!" And he added, "What a bore this Leibl fellow must be, what a mentality and how slow!" The attitude of Leibl when confronted with Böcklin's *Centaurs* is no less characteristic, "Creatures like that don't exist," snapped Leibl.

These two judgments sum up in a dramatic way the aesthetic points of view which prevailed towards the end of the nineteenth century and we can recognize the twin currents—the realist and the fantastic—which, at this period, underline their contradictions in Romanticism itself. In point of fact, realism and symbolism had always got on happily together in preceding centuries. Their conflict in the nineteenth is, moreover, more apparent than real. If Böcklin, the champion of the idealistic Post-Romanticism, invents, he invariably employs elements of the real; he is rarely fantastic in the true sense of the word.

Furthermore the realists were never fettered to a lazy, purblind objectivity. In this Leibl, whom Böcklin saw as the champion of a loathesome naturalism, existed a modest lyricism, a hidden poetry which sang in a whisper. Definitions should therefore take more account of these subtleties.

REALISM

The advent of pictorial realism corresponds, as far as the aesthetic angle is concerned, to active changes that were taking place in German society; the conception of a Germany unified around imperialism, mechanical progress, new interest in social problems, and that growth of materialism which increased wealth and the "will to power," whose imperatives were formulated by Nieztsche, inevitably bring in their train, all bore on the immediate present. The wish to react against Romantic unreality which threatened to become a formula stimulated this urge to find a new outlet; the presence of Courbet and Millet in the all-important Munich Exibition of 1869, that vital turning point of German aestheticism, imposed French realism as a model.

This realism could present very divergent aspects. The religious naturalism of Fritz von Uhde (1848-1911), reverting to the custom favored by the Old Masters of ignoring local color and dressing Biblical characters according to the fashions of their own time, aimed at bringing about a renewal of sacred art. It is an obvious reaction against the theatrical emphasis of the historical painters and the arbitrary "literalness" of the Hungarian, Munkaczy (1844-1909) or the English painter Alma Tadema who aimed at exact archeological reconstructions of the ancient East. Uhde's ingenuous and moving idea of setting Christ at the table of Saxon peasants was, on occasion, responsible for intense and forceful works, but he remained an isolated phenomenon. In the realm of religious art, this sympathetic return to truth implied the abandonment of the slavish imitation of the Middle Ages and Renaissance, dear to the Nazarenes, which we still see persisting in that "delayed Nazarene" of the Tyrol, Franz Stecher (1814-1853) who took orders, then abandoned the priesthood, led an adventurous life in America and died at the age of thirty-nine. His enormous frescoes and oils in the churches of Austria and Pennsylvania express the tender and sincere depth of piety, the almost childlike candor which Stecher revealed on every human countenance. A late Romantic, Stecher returns at the same time to great Baroque decoration and religious art which went far beyond Uhde's naturalism into the symbolic Primitivism of the Worpswede School which was one of the most successful movements for the revival of sacred art.

While certain monasteries, such as that of Beuron, steered this revival in the direction of the first Renaissance, resulting finally in a kind of neo-Nazarenism, the Worpswede group began by proposing a return to nature, comparable to that of the Flemish at Laethem-St. Martin, and the Bavarians at Dachau. The painters of Worpswede who set up by the noble, yet severe landscape of the North Sea in 1894, avoided city life, with its bustle and artificiality. It became the meeting place of very different artists—Carl Vinnen (1863-1922), Otto Modersohn (1865-1943) and his wife Paula Modersohn-Becker, who occupies an important niche in the Expressionist movement. They included poets (Rilke was there for some time), and a kind of pantheistic Christianity with a flavor of community life after the Fourier pattern lent a certain unity to the works of this School, and a family air that cannot be found to an equal degree in other Schools, Dachau for example. The mixture here of the social and religious elements assumed a more authentic note than is observable in von Uhde's pious scenes of peasant life. The common ambition which brought together Fritz Overbeck, Hans am Ende, Fritz Mackensen, Heinrich Vogeler, who aimed at living and working according to the absolute of truth, was to replace Uhde's ideas with a genuine naturalism. The soul of the land and sea, the pantheistic religion which unites individuals to the elements, were all evoked, not always unaccompanied by "literature," but never without a great deal of good faith.

The painting of historical subjects, in reaction to the conventional travesties which Romanticism imposed on the people and episodes of the past, demanded "local color" in its turn, the first inspiration having come from Belgians such as Biefve and Gallait, and the Frenchmen, Delaroche and Delacroix. The artists hunted out old customs, weapons and other properties in public and private collections and junk shops. Karl von Piloty (1826-1886) with his persuasive tongue and the dramatic vivacity of his compositions seemed something new and intriguing at that time, that is before he lapsed into academism[22].

With Franz von Lenbach (1836-1904) portrait painting, nurtured on the striking lesson of truth that Courbet taught, was happily wedded to an abundant facility and eclecticism which bore this painter to the very pinnacle of Wilhelm I's Germany, all of whose great men, from Wagner to Bismarck, he portrayed. Without any real originality, for he plagiarized from Rembrandt, Van Dyck, and Reynolds, Lenbach often achieved a certain sobriety, though it did not extend to an interpretation of inner life—remaining, as he did, the official portraitist of an epoch and a country. He was capable of a lyrical impulse and fused into his best pictures the intense and communicative life of the eyes which is, as we have now discovered more than once, the constant of the German portrait.

He is not as great as Wilhelm Leibl, Wilhelm Trübner and Max Slevogt, who had the honor of having started a School. The Exhibition of 1869 in which the "refusés" of the French Salon emerged victors, provided the occasion for Courbet and Leibl (1844-1900) to admire each other's works and for Leibl to take cognizance of the strong originality of this sober and vigorous realism. Leibl went back to nature with all the sympathetic power of a lyrical temperament which imposes discipline on itself in order to stay within the limits of objectivity, but which discovers in this very objectivity the resources of an intimate rural and woodland poetry, imbued with a self-critical attitude of unusual efficacity. The scent of wet shrubs, the rough texture of peasants' clothes in terms of paint quality and color are comparable to the artist's masterly treatment of flesh. His conception of realism is less literary than Courbet's and Millet's because it is completely free of social implications[23].

Karl Haider (1846-1922), must be accorded a place apart in German landscape at this period. This curious and remarkable artist was a pupil of Ludwig Richter and is a link with the Romantics. It is significant that one of his finest pictures bears for its title a line of Goethe, "Über allen Gipfel ist Ruh..." (Munich, 1896). A friend and fellow pupil of Leibl's, fond of Italy and an admirer of Böcklin, Haider forged a new vision for himself, a virgin sensibility, ready to experience nature in all its freshness. His training as a musician (his father wanted him to be a singer) added to the purely plastic and poetic qualities of his pictures a harmony which imbues his landscape with a moving grace.

As opposed to what is popularly thought, Wilhelm Trübner (1851-1917), strongly impressed by Courbet whom he discovered when he was eighteen and by Leibl with whom he worked after 1871, is a better landscape painter than portraitist. The vigorous and triturated paint of the *Portrait of the Girl with Folded Hands* (Dresden, 1878) is an original contribution and a notable step forward, and along with the warm color which animates the solid paint, compels our admiration. But the best of Trübner is in the *Schloss Hemsbach* (Munich, 1907) with its glow of iridescent lights which lend a lyric note to the façade of the house, the vibration of the foliage and the distant mystery of the undergrowth. Nearer Manet than Courbet, Max Slevogt (1868-1932), who combines the swift facility of the illustrator with the artificial brightness of the stage-designer, seems superficial.

THE IMPRESSIONISTS

Is there such a thing as "German Impressionism"? It is begging the question to put the words in quotation marks. We can however recognize that when the Exhibition of 1879, ten years after that of the Realists, won German admiration for the French Impressionists, whom their compatriots scorned and refused to acknowledge, the interest was very great on the part of artists and connoisseurs. In contrast to what happened a decade before, however, the 1879 Exhibition did not create a movement comparable with that of the Realists, probably because the aesthetic principles of the Impressionists awoke less response among German painters whose "pleinairisme" was nearer that of a Rousseau, a Daubigny or a Corot. The liberation of brushwork, the seizing of the fugitive moment and its fragile magic were part of a too specifically French phenomenon, perhaps, to create a school on the other bank of the Rhine.

Among those whom we call German Impressionists, not one is so in the sense in which that term can be applied to Monet, Sisley, Pissarro. Manet and, to a lesser degree, Degas, influenced men like Theodor Hagen (1842-1919), and if Adolf Menzel adopted some part of Impressionist technique, he did not apply it to landscape but to genre painting. Menzel (1815-1905) allied Meissonier's historical realism to a brilliant craftsmanship and this has won him a celebrity which the French find it difficult to account for. Having become a realist towards the end of his life and fallen under the spell of the picturesque aspects of working class life and the factory, he secured a niche as a versatile and skillful minor master, successful in everything he undertook but lacking the ambition of genius.

Almost the same thing can be said of the painter who is sometimes haled as the "German Impressionist," Max Liebermann (1847-1919). This cultured artist of cosmopolitan tastes experimented with Belgian and Dutch Neo-Realism and French Impressionism by turns without ever taking the matter very far. A fundamental respectability, a rather cold seriousness and somewhat mechanical handling of paint, plus a timid hesitation when confronted with the potentialities of light, made Liebermann an excellent transitional artist. A discreet poetry, which he is reluctant to admit, not infrequently animates his objectivity.

Impressionism could probably have served as a new means of expression for imagination and Romantic sensibility, but the latter was too closely linked to symbolism in this second half of the nineteenth century when realism and idealism meet. Warmly welcomed, understood, freely introduced into galleries and private collections, Impressionism nevertheless remained on the periphery of German art. The latter had other problems to settle and its interior development imposed contradictory solutions suggested by the perception and expression of reality—the subordination of the image to the idea or the submission to strict objectivity. While these conflicts were in progress, a compromise between objective reality and imagination assumed very varied aspects among the painters whom we may call Post-Romantics.

THE POST-ROMANTICS

WHATEVER the label we give to various tendencies, all of which are directed against realism (Symbolism, Neo-Romanticism, Lyrical Realism, Plastic Idealism), they possess, over and above their characteristics, a common trait which links them to one of the aspects of Romanticism, the constant in the development of German art and which we are to find again in the next century in the so-called *Neue-Sachlichkeit* (New Objectivity) movement. At no period in the history of German art does there exist a divorce between objectivity and subjectivity; their marriage is indissoluble.

Among the Post-Romantics at the end of the nineteenth century love of objects in their humble truth charges the latter with an intense and quiet beauty, a spiritualized emotion which, moreover, already existed below the surface in Von Uhde's pious naturalism. To define the work of Hans Thoma (1839-1924), the most remarkable representative of what we might call "Lyrical Realism" we have to fall back on the title Goethe gave his memoirs, *Dichtung und Wahrheit* (Poetry and Truth) Hans Thoma's landscapes are neither dreams nor reconstructions nor transpositions but records faithfully, affectionately put down on the canvas. The painter brings the same piety with which Von Uhde's peasants welcome Christ to their family table to his representation of a clump of trees, an open valley, a village whose factories send up curls of smoke at twilight. He is more or less insensitive to the mythological aspect of natural forces; he has no need to think of the great god Pan, before he can be aware of the breath of the Spirit on the chosen spots of his native Black Forest. The reproach has been made against him that it is a spirit geared down to this rustic, somewhat bourgeois sensibility, and that Hans Thoma may be thought of as a philistine; and it is true that this specifically German *Gemütlichkeit* is imperfectly understood, if indeed at all, especially abroad. This rather naive serenity sometimes veils the true greatness of a modest art whose eloquence lies precisely in this silent contemplation of untroubled space. The *Open Valley* (Frankfurt), the *Taunus* (Munich, 1881), *The Waterfall* of 1880, provide a better definition of the talent and aspirations of this miller's son who had learned the rudiments of his art from a painter of clock dials, than his genre paintings, skillfully constructed though they often were, or his portraits which possess affinities with those of his friend Leibl. If Hans Thoma's landscapes are lacking in that secret and evocative note familiar to us in those of Haider whom he met in Florence and admired, they present an "opening-up" of feeling comparable to those open valleys contemplated from above which are the most successful expressions of that charming heart.

Compared with Hans Thoma's muted music, the symphonies of the Basle painter Arnold Böcklin (1827-1901) stun us with their fanfares and din. This artist has suffered from the discredit into which "program painting" has fallen. Because he never painted a picture whose *contents* he did not deem indispensable, we have lost sight of the considerable merits of a painter who, to be a pure painter, only needed to disassociate himself from music and literature. Böcklin is romantic even in this aim of uniting the three forms of expression in painting itself. In this he was going further than the Romantics themselves and pursuing an unattainable ideal. This man of inexhaustible vitality plunged back into the very spring of primitive life which he felt in a direct and full-blooded way, even if later in his painting he gave it the appearance of a mythological divinity. He never stopped painting except to go for long country walks or play the compositions of old Italian masters on his har-

HANS THOMA – SUMMER-PLEASURE. 1905 – (0,845; 0,715) WALLRAF-RICHARTZ-MUSEUM, COLOGNE

monium. He would stop for hours on the seashore watching the succession of breaking waves. This descendant of the Humanists was a very cultured man—hence perhaps the excess of themes borrowed from Greek mythology and the fact that he was unable to separate nature from myths, paint the sea without tritons, rocks at midday without showing Pan asleep on them. The thought of death weighed heavily on him and he worked rapidly as if his years were numbered (actually he died at Fiesole, almost an octogenarian) and he was often discovered in a state of collapse in front of his easel. Panic fear, the obsession with the skeleton, war, plagues, graveyards (he painted nine versions of *The Isle of the Dead*) had a fascination for this powerful, vigorous and sensual man, in spite of himself. He could moreover display an exquisite delicacy of feeling and color, not least in the different versions of the *Honeymoon in Italy;* there we see a very different Böcklin from the one whom the fanatics of "painting without subject" abominate and jeer at. It is easy to be unjust to him, for his very work invites it. But we should remember that his pictures are completely free of affectation and insincerity. He was an "idyllic" (he insisted on having his studio filled with flowers); he *lived* his mythology which has nothing bookish about it for him, and some of his full-size compositions such as *The Besieged Town* in Düsseldorf, are heightened by a visionary passion.

If it were insincere, Arnold Böcklin's work would be vile and repulsive, above all if the intrusion of literature interfered with the painter's craftsmanship; fortunately this urge to create only served to increase the number of his happy inventions. Nature lives and breathes in them. Böcklin stood up in the middle of the waves in order to note their transparency and ripples, and his studies have the careful exactness of those of Caspar David Friedrich. Some of his contemporaries considered the realism of his tritons vulgar and objected to his famous Basle painting because "it smelled of fish"; it is the highest praise, I think, that one could give it.

For the same reason we should exonerate Anselm Feuerbach (1829-1880) from the reproach habitually brought against the Post-Romantics—and the Romantics too—of doing "literary" painting. Because he attired his beautiful Italian wife as a heroine of ancient history and mythology, he is criticized for his liking for "subject." Feuerbach had been Schadow's pupil in Düsseldorf and Rahl's in Munich; subsequently he fell under the spell of Rubens in Antwerp and Paris and of Tintoretto and Veronese in Venice. His ambition was to rival them and he aspired to cover with classical compositions spaces which he would people with his Hellenic dreams. In this he was encouraged by that fascinating character who exercised a decisive influence on the painting of the second half of the nineteenth century—the collector Adolf Friedrich von Schack, whose house has become a museum. Schack bought the Romantics and gave Franz Lenbach early encouragement in his difficult start. The romantic tastes of Schack, who was also interested in his contemporaries, naturally attracted him to those who were linked with the Romantics of the first half of the century. He collected assiduously, sometimes indiscriminately, but he was on sure ground when he concentrated his attention on the trio, indisputably the best, Arnold Böcklin, Hans von Marées and Anselm Feuerbach who were still unknown. The Schack Gallery in Munich is a well-deserved homage to the foresight of this patron.

Feuerbach's name can be coupled with that of Couture whose pupil he was during his time in Paris; in his case too, we are presented with an artificial and interpreted Greece. Ill-equipped for the great, monumental decorations which he had to renounce, unable to cope with compositions overloaded with figures, he gave his best work in the portraits he did from his wife *Nanna Risi*, or in classical episodes, treated, without setting or theatricality, for their dramatic significance, such as his *Medea* (Munich 1870).

Among these poet-painters whose poetry is inseparable from their painting, the Swiss Albert Welti (1862-1912) who had been Böcklin's pupil, deserves special attention. Welti is a second-rank painter but an agreeable and picturesque artist. A sober interpreter of the peasant genre scene, a lyrical realist, he possessed neither the Schumannesque effusiveness of Hans Thoma nor the intrepid exuberance of Böcklin.

The problems presented by Max Klinger's work are complex and numerous, first because Klinger (1857-1920) was a sculptor as much as a painter, and of doubtful aesthetic principles—witness his enthusiasm for polychromatic statues such as the notorious *Beethoven*. The bad taste of the Wilhelm II period repercussed on this original artist of manifold gifts which he made the mistake of dissipating. Advancing further in religious realism than Von Uhde, he executed his famous *Crucifixion* (Leipzig) with a brutal, almost repellent truth to life which aroused heated arguments, since Klinger had introduced contemporaries in strange states of dress and undress in this sacred scene of which he had made a realistic "slice of life." He pursued the fantastic reveries of a visionary in the engravings which recount the metamorphoses of a woman's glove lost at a ball; he transposed Brahms' symphonies. Yet he is full of humanitarian aspirations, and in opaque paint which brings the bodies down to earth, he attempted a clumsy reconciliation between paganism and Christianity by putting *Christ in Olympus*, the theme of one of his most ambitious compositions (Vienna, 1897). This acceptance of physical ugliness—his testimony of our sad human condition—this insistence on banishing any gleam of holiness even from the most heart-rending Bible episodes, his sensual charm in *The Source* (Dresden, 1892), prosaic with its dark, heavy flesh tones while the flower-starred meadow and distant hills are delightfully painted, sum up the paradoxical character of this tormented artist.

Among the young Post-Romantics or Neo-Romantics in whom Schack took an interest, Hans von Marées (1837-1887), despite his predilection for scenes taken from mythology or antiquity, occupies a place apart. In Germany Hellenism does not lead to Classicism; on the contrary, it arouses the idiosyncrasies of romanticism. In France classical feeling is literary, theatrical and Davidian. For the Germans, on the other hand, to think Greece means searching out a road of one's own inner Greece. Hans von Marées discovered antiquity in Italy and after his first stay in Rome his manner underwent a radical transformation. His contact with Italian landscape, the antique sculpture of the Vatican and Michelangelo awoke in him

ANSELM FEUERBACH – NANNA.
1861 – (0,74; 0,55) WALLRAF-
RICHARTZ-MUSEUM, COLOGNE

a nostalgia for a serene and mysterious antiquity. In a completely natural way he worked out his technique in thick, somber paint substance, illuminated with red and gold reflections. Antiquity was shrouded in a mist like the emanation from the primal clay from which the figures of Rembrandt, whom Marées studied assiduously, also emerged. If we object to a certain monotony in his constant use of reddish browns, we must admit that these handsome, dreamy figures are disposed in accordance with truly classical laws of rhythm and harmony. The Greek gods who people Marées' pictures are like Böcklin's, spirits of the earth and forest, stripped of their conventional attributes and become forces which we sense rather than see.

The Bernese Ferdinand Hodler (1853-1918) has also a mythology all his own, but his landscapes are inhabited more by symbols than by gods. Several tendencies

HANS VON MAREES – DIANA RESTING. 1863 – (0,95; 1,34)
BAYERISCHE STAATSGEMÄLDESAMMLUNGEN, MUNICH

are to be observed in this rich and versatile personality—the creator of full scale wall decorations in which all the civic splendor and full panoply of war of medieval Switzerland are revived, the landscape painter sensitive to the vibration of light. Naked figures, drawn with a somewhat puritanical dryness, often stroll through his landscapes. Symbolic art, according to Hodler, should suggest not the state of being but of becoming, not immobility but the passage and the transition, not the attitude but the movement, the totality and the infinite. His device was—eye, reason, heart. Of Hodler we can say that he is an eye strolling through the valleys, mountains and past the lakes of his native land. He lacked the exile mentality of Böcklin, Feuerbach and Marées who fled to Italy, lived and died there. Nor did he need to introduce passion into nature to raise it to the level of his own emotion. When there are no symbolic personages in his landscapes, the powerful breath of invisible beings seems to take their place. His mountains are peopled with those Panic forces that unleash catastrophes *(The Avalanche*, Solothurn).

In the classicism of symbolic compositions such as the *Eurythmy* and the *Disillusioned Souls* (Berne) we catch a hint of Carstens or perhaps William Blake, and, at the same time, a feeling of construction behind his arrangement of the figures in a colonnade fashion, even when, as in the *Disillusioned Souls*, the artist aimed at representing the "unappeasable despair in front of life."

Peopling the landscape with symbols does not mean the indiscriminate introduction of allegories but an interpretation of nature's message to man's soul through plastic and pictorial means. Ferdinand Hodler achieved his result more laboriously than Giovanni Segantini (1858-1899) who does not, strictly speaking, belong to German painting since he was born in Trentino, but who exercised a considerable influence on the origins of Expressionism. When he entitled his representations of distant glaciers, plateaus of wind-swept peaks, deserted meadows, *Becoming or Decline*, he was evoking that "tragedy of the landscape" which took a very different form with Caspar David Friedrich. His color, without being arbitrary and systematic, aims at being allegorical, and the light which floods his vast panoramas is intended to reveal the power and joy of God. Pantheistic after the manner of a man of the mountains who lives in close intimacy with the elements, Segantini dreamed, like the old Chinese painters, of enclosing in a single picture a vast space to express the feeling of infinity.

At the head of Austrian Symbolism which inspired the Viennese *Sezession* of 1897 Gustav Klimt appeared in an anti-realist movement along with Ferdinand Hodler and Edvard Munch. There is little aesthetic affinity between the Norwegian painter and Klimt, except that they both turn their backs on realism with the same determination. But, whereas Munch, who was to be one of the "fathers" of Expressionism, moved in the direction of dramatic symbolism, the Viennese painter, who had been the pupil of Makart, was eager to carry out large-scale decorations. He started by working with his brother Ernst and Franz Matsch on theater *décor* and murals of vast dimensions. But what in Makart was pomposity, exuberance and often vulgarity was refined by the tormented personality of Klimt who was animated by intellectual ambitions. Overcharged with "meaning" as they are, the paintings of the Viennese are characterized by his insistence—very modern in 1897—on renouncing the illusions of perspective and all realism of form and color. Klimt created a refined plastic language, even precious and excessively distorted, with the primary aim of combating the coarseness of naturalism. It is in his portraits and landscape that his art seems certain to survive. If the "modern style" aspect of Klimt's symbolist pictures is far removed from present-day taste, the determination to treat the picture as a colored surface, to divide that surface into small colored areas whose tones interact with the iridescent vivacity of oriental clothes, to practice an arrogant unreality, counts in his favor. It explains why he influenced the young Kandinsky and how the taproots of the *Blaue Reiter* are, paradoxically enough, buried in the artificial compost of the *Jugendstil.*

Side by side with Klimt and his successors we encounter the equally strange personality of Egon Schiele (1890-1918) who takes this decorative unreality, known as the *Sezession*, to its highest point of eccentricity and perhaps artificiality. In this painter, destined to die very young, lay all the potentiality of a wholesale renewal which, alas, he did not have time to accomplish; his way of enclosing form in a circular line which attracts rhythmic currents, smooth and as it were chalky backgrounds against which stand out figures of complicated arabesques, and the almost abstract beauty of the *Autumn Tree* (1912) are an eloquent testimony to an exuberant and tragic personality.

Klimt's and Schiele's symbolism often contains morbid and macabre elements, the seed of which can already be discerned in the extremely strange painting of the very uneven Gabriel Cornelius von Max (1840-1915), who was born in Prague, received his training in Vienna and died in Munich. Max wavers between historical realism in the manner of Piloty, who was his professor in 1863, and visionary realism which has won him the esteem of modern surrealists. Max's work is bathed in mystery, either because the enigmatic faces he paints resemble superimposed masks, behind which the unknown face lies hidden, or because his personages are engaged in enigmatic actions. The picture entitled *Clairvoyant, or the Second Face* (Munich) and his *Mushroom-peeler* (Munich) are surrounded by an ambiguous atmosphere in which reality is merely an allusion to some invisible process by which the being is made and unmade. The term "symbolism" does not apply in von Max's case or, at any rate, the symbols he expresses can never be clearly interpreted. He reminds us of an even more nebulous Maeterlinck.

The *Jugendstil*, rather than stemming from true symbolism, is a deliberate *unreality*, an art which broke away from tradition and is to be found chiefly in the applied arts, impinging on the plastic arts only in their minor forms—the poster, book illustration, the ceramic statue. When we see the simultaneous appearance of the *Jugendstil* in Germany, with its Viennese "branch" of the *Sezession* style, the Liberty style in England, the Modern style in France, we realize that we must consider the vast extent of this extremely homogeneous movement in its aspirations and means of expression, as a "period phenomenon" with a social no less than aesthetic importance.

In the *Jugendstil* which its opposition to realism defines as a kind of extension of Post-Romanticism or Neo-Romanticism, examples of plastic and applied art interact and exercise a mutual influence on each other. Characteristic of it is the desire for unity of style in which everything from architecture down to the most insignificant household accessory—a door handle—is viewed as a unified and complete creation, brought about in accordance with the same imperatives. The picture which found a place in this complex in which aesthetics, decoration and craftsmanship were all equally involved, was inspired by the same spirit, and in its turn inspired the decorative artists. The celebrated house of the Bavarian painter Franz von Stuck (1863-1928) provides the best example. From the symbolic and mythological realism of Böcklin, who was his master in 1885, down to the launching of the review *Jugend*, the manifesto of the movement, to which it gave its name, and the erection of the famous Villa Stuck in 1890, the sanctuary of the *Jugendstil*, Franz von Stuck himself developed towards the paradoxical notion of the total work of art, experienced by Runge and the Romantics as a sacred phenomenon and realized in *Merzism* by Kurt Schwitters, becoming in him something extra-pictorial. Stuck's mythological compositions (*Battles of Fauns*, Munich, 1889, or of *Amazons*, Munich, 1897) are violent, rather

FERDINAND HODLER – THE AVALANCHE. 1887 – (1,30; 0,99) SOLOTHURN MUSEUM, PROPERTY OF THE SWISS CONFEDERATION

portentous, inspired by an occasionally rustic Hellenism which has none of the sentiment of the sacred to be found in Böcklin and Marées.

At the same period as Stuck was working on the floral decorations which were to win him a Gold Medal at the Universal Exhibition of 1900 in Paris—the "Métro" style having recognized a brother in the *Jugendstil*—bolder painters exaggerated this anti-naturalism still further and took it to its logical extreme—Abstraction. Line, now become autonomous, existing in its own right, a pure arabesque that was soon to renounce the plant-resemblance that it had first adopted, interpreted pure rhythmic movement for its own sake. Hans Schmithals' compositions (b. 1878), more advanced, more resolutely non-figurative even than those of Hermann Obrist (1863-1927) whose studio he frequented, opened up an unexpected road. A student of natural science at Heidelberg, before devoting himself to painting and the decorative arts, Obrist achieved that reduction of form which in the same year, 1900, transformed the woodcarving of Richard Riemerschmied and the stylized volutes of Fritz Endell into a play of abstract curves.

The *Jugendstil* painters such as Leo Putz, Hugo von Habermann and Fritz Erler who enjoyed their hour of fame in the conflict of enthusiasm and disapproval accorded this "revolutionary" style (in 1900), affected the development of German art less than the decorators did; in Obrist and Schmithals existed, in substance, ideals which were to come into full bloom in the aesthetic theories of the *Blaue Reiter* and even the *Bauhaus*.

THE MAIN TRENDS IN THE TWENTIETH CENTURY

The word *Sezession* which recurs continually at the beginning of the century, a rallying cry which brought groups of painters together whether for a temporary exhibition or permanent activity, is the characteristic vocable of the determination to break with tradition that is common to these very divergent movements. Even in the "schools"—associations of short duration, quickly dissolved because they are not founded on a true community of aims but fortuitous intimacies, any kind of unity is lacking—every artist remains enclosed within his own uncompromising personality. This is so even when a common language inclines us to believe in a common inspiration in the groups inspired by the desire to get back to the land again—*Die Scholle* (the Soil), the guiding principles of which are roughly the same as those of the School of Laethem-Saint-Martin in Belgium, and the School of Worpswede from which emerged what we may call a symbolist naturalism.

It was the city of Munich which started the *Sezession* movement in 1892. The first Berlin *Sezession*, with Max Liebermann as its president, was created seven years later. Slevogt and Corinth exhibited there for the first time, and Hodler made his first appearance there in Germany. These exhibitions had the same power of revelation and leavening that the years 1869 and 1879 had possessed. The Exhibition of French Impressionists of 1902, in Berlin and Munich, was to accentuate the importance as a turning point of 1902, the year when Leibl and Böcklin died and Meier-Graefe's article on Van Gogh appeared which was destined to have enormous consequences on the development of Expressionism. In Vienna, too, the 1900 *Sezession* and the decoration of Klimt at the University, inaugurated a "modern" movement, parallel to that of the *Jugendstil* of similar tendencies.

EXPRESSIONISM

This determination to make a break, responsible for the *Sezessions*, turned Expressionism into a categoric reaction against the forms of expression of the preceding century. It is impossible to define Expressionism as such because it does not correspond to any single aesthetic principle but several, and because we cannot reduce the strong personalities whom it is customary to group under this label to a common denominator. As opposed to the French Impressionists, they do not constitute a real "stylistic family" and nothing could be vaguer, more fluid than the meaning

LOVIS CORINTH – WALCHENSEE. 1921 – (0,70; 0,85)
BAYERISCHE STAATSGEMÄLDESAMMLUNGEN, MUNICH

of this title. Let us however recall the definition made by Grohmann who sees in Expressionism "an artistic idiom which, following on Impressionism, restores human drama to the picture and, in the place of the most rational canon of forms, with its equilibrium of colored sensations, sets up an irrational one." The novelty of this artistic procedure rests in the fact that nature and the painter's representation of it meet about half-way, that in the reality which he perceives, the painter incorporates, in advance, the representation of it, as he imagines it to be, and that he has already transformed nature before picking up brush or pencil. Van Gogh's famous saying "Color expresses something by itself; it cannot be dispensed with, it must be exploited; what is good is right," became a rallying cry and an aesthetic precept for the Expressionists.

But the painters are united much more by a spirit of revolt and a zeal to express their individual and unique message than by a common discipline.

Lovis Corinth (1858-1925) is one of these painters, poised between the nineteenth and twentieth centuries, whom it is most difficult to define, for none of the terms one would employ entirely meets his case nor contains his forcible personality, extremely modern in form and spirit, energetically and almost brutally expressionistic before the event, yet rooted in that Post-Romanticism in which Böcklin and Hans von Marées had stood side by side. The work of Lovis Corinth, with its provoking sensuality which affects more vulgarity than it in fact possesses—a challenge as it were to the middle-class philistines of Wilhelm II's Germany—realistic in subject but showing a freedom of treatment which transforms every painting into a dramatic adventure of the artist struggling with the means of expression which take him on to destinations of which he was not aware, bursts through all traditions. In one stride Corinth advanced further than all his contemporaries in the direction of explosion of form, chromatism freed from every subordination to the element of representation. He abolishes the traditions of perspective and construction, for every picture, every landscape is a new experience that has no successor. The disorder in which these elements meet and war on each other is the reflection of a tormented conscience and a superhuman aspiration to recreate the world in accordance with the dictates of his own imagination. It must have been early in his career that Corinth came across Cézanne whose initial work was more accessible than the constructive canvases (his painting, too, was "blobby"!) and he probably recognized a kindred spirit in Van Gogh. The profound gulf which first became evident in 1911 between the Liebermann impressionism that he first practiced and the proto-expressionism dating from that year, is reputed to have been caused by an attack of apoplexy, affecting his vision. It seems a possiblity. This change to a visionary kind of impressionism which occurred then does not correspond to a pathological phenomenon in the normal sense of the term, but to an aesthetic transformation precipitated by an external accident. So it came about that Corinth now brought to bear on the landscape, imbued with tragedy, the dramatic passion which had inspired such compositions as his *Ecce Homo* of Basle, a mixture of anguished humanity and social satire. It almost justified Liebermann's complaint, "Corinth goes to the very frontier of the grotesque." The excess in his feelings, his way of distorting natural forms, of hurling color wholesale on the canvas in a kind of frenzy of joy, painful in its intensity *(Walchensee,* Munich, 1921) breaks every rule, substitutes hallucination for perception, intuitive tumult for ordered reason.

DIE BRÜCKE

THE painters who, in 1903, founded the group called *Die Brücke* ("The Bridge") round which gathered—with fruitful results—the strongest personalities of the early days of Expressionism, could with justification have claimed Lovis Corinth as their "father." In the first years of the century *Die Brücke* had the enormously fertilizing influence which the *Blaue Reiter* movement was to exercise ten years afterwards, and, a decade later, the *Bauhaus.* To start with *Die Brücke* consisted mainly of Erich Heckel, Ernst Ludwig Kirchner and Karl Schmidt-Rottluff, the founder-members. Later, in 1906, they were joined by Emil Nolde and Max Pechstein and by Otto Müller in 1910. The group was disbanded in 1913 on the brink of the European War, at the conclusion of which the second Expressionist wave was to surge up, but it possessed no real cohesion; Nolde and Pechstein had already broken away. These painters shared a certain conception of the representation of the real in the sense that, for them, the independence of the image and the autonomy of subjectivity took precedence even over the existence of the object itself. Taking the object whose intrinsic reality, no less than spatial realism and concordance of form and color, was indifferent to them as their point of departure, they invented a new world. Self-taught for the most part, they also invented their technique and in their pictures preserve only those relations with the truth of the subjects treated that their determination to start "from scratch" allowed. Their metaphysical uneasiness constituted the primordial source of a violently anti-naturalist creation, since expression is the sole justification of a work of art—expression being the product of the imagination which rethinks the visible world by turning its back on it. The color-orchestration—and here there is a resemblance with the Fauves—deliberately neglected the reference to nature practiced by the Impressionists; the artist insisted on the picture composing itself as spontaneously and immediately as possible, he being the transcriber of the emotion in its raw state on the virgin canvas. Each picture is a convulsive projection, a state of consciousness of extreme tension, often haunted by morbid obsessions, affecting reality after the manner of dreams which, after all, possess a logic of their own. Their pictorial idiom was also strongly influenced by the technique of wood engraving which gives their drawing the acid hardness, the arbitrary simplification of volumes, the depth of line to be found in the almost ferocious accentuation of the figures, which are their common characteristics.

The landscapes of Erich Heckel (1883), with their contrasts of pure colors, boldly combined, illustrate better than those of any other painter this nature convulsed by volcanic movements, echoes of those which shake the artist's soul—nature in the midst of which the Expressionist painter situates himself in order to capture its tremors and recount their wild splendor. At the same time Heckel endeavors to lay hold of the crystal, which is the result and justification of the cataclysms that have occurred in the depths of the crucible where the elements have fused together. More effectively than his nudes, they translate the desperate desire to rediscover the state of original innocence which the crystal symbolizes. Heckel's method is to contemplate trees and mountains with the wondering innocence one might have had when the world first dawned, with all the immediacy of a contact uncontaminated by any preconceived idea, any preoccupation with style and representation. It is this which lends nature, as seen and expressed by him, that grandiose and solemn manner of detaching itself from man and dominating him.

Co-founder of *Die Brücke*, impelled in emulation of Gauguin towards the mirages of tropical Eden, Max Pechstein (1881), lived several years preceding the 1914 War on the island of Palau, but it was not the paradisiac, sensual liberty which Gauguin had experienced there which re-appears in this painter's work, for Pechstein recognized in the stylizations of Polynesian art a constructive principle comparable to that which the Cubists discovered in African masks.

Otto Müller (1874-1930) also came under the influence of Gauguin but not to the extent of setting off for Tahiti. His favorite models are gypsies, all angles, or weighed down with animal melancholy. His acid and bitter Arcadia, dominated by gray-greens and subtle blacks, follows, it seems, the example of Egyptian funeral frescoes which he considered a high form of art, and even his sensuality finds pleasure in a perverse ugliness.

More varied and more difficult to situate, Christian Rohlfs (1849-1938) was over fifty years of age when *Die Brücke* was founded; he embarked on Expressionism after numerous artistic experiments and some years of Impressionism in the style of Liebermann, and in his later life he was to attain a quality of abstraction which was foreshadowed in 1912 when he painted his *Soest Cathedral*, a subject which also inspired Feininger.

The youngest of the founders of *Die Brücke*—he was almost forty years younger than Rohlfs—Karl Schmidt-Rottluff (b. 1884) differs from the majority of the Expres-

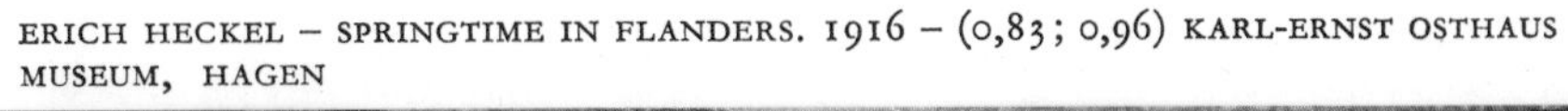
ERICH HECKEL – SPRINGTIME IN FLANDERS. 1916 – (0,83; 0,96) KARL-ERNST OSTHAUS MUSEUM, HAGEN

sionists in his preoccupation with formal, almost Cézannesque construction; for him landscape is no longer merely a dramatic outburst on the part of the elements; a rational need for order, plastic equilibrium which links him with Cubism, is mingled with the autonomy of the image.

If Paula Modersohn-Becker (1876-1907) did not, strictly speaking, belong to *Die Brücke*, she was, technically, near enough, but her spiritual preoccupations, her aspiration for a more natural life than that led by the painters in the art centers, Munich, Dresden or Berlin, an aspiration which, it was said, led her to Worpswede, gave her a place apart in Expressionism. Her anxious temperament, perceptible in her letters, drew her to Rilke whom she got to know in his retreat by the Baltic. Dying, at the early age of thirty, too soon for her talent to come to full fruition, she had not entirely thrown off the influence of Cézanne and Gauguin whom she had carefully studied during her many stays in Paris (1900, 1903, 1905). Her portraits have a resigned, melancholy look, as if they were seeking the spectator's sympathy, and if her color has the same brilliant and warm violence as that of the *Die Brücke* painters, a kind of symbolism corresponding to a certain latent mysticism is observable.

EMIL NOLDE – THE LEGEND OF ST. MARY OF EGYPT: AT THE PORT OF ALEXANDRIA. 1912 – (0,86; 1,00) KUNSTHALLE, HAMBURG

EMIL NOLDE – MARSHLAND. 1916 – (0,735; 1,005) KUNSTMUSEUM, BASLE

EMIL NOLDE

The case of Emil Nolde (1867-1956) is a strange one; his field of experience included journeys to the Far East and close contact with the *Blaue Reiter* painters whose outlook he shared after leaving *Die Brücke*. In point of fact, he did not participate in any group for he was the victim of his shy and wild temperament which finds an outlet in his painting in a kind of delirium which whirls away personages, objects and even landscape as in a cyclone. This external vehemence has its counterpart, where his intimate religious feelings are concerned, in his urge to treat the most paradoxical and scabrous episodes in the lives of the saints. This is particularly noticeable in the triptych of the *Legend of St. Mary of Egypt* (Hamburg, 1912) in which we find side by side with the idiom of the medieval polyptych a primitive crudity, mingling sacred and burlesque elements in a manner we also

ERNST LUDWIG KIRCHNER – HUT IN THE ALPS. 1917 – (1,21; 1,50) STAATLICHE KUNSTHALLE, KARLSRUHE

encounter, to a lesser extent, in another great religious painter of our time, the French Expressionist Georges Rouault.

In order to experience the authentic and shattering religious emotion which emanates from these paintings by Nolde—which throw convention and tradition to the winds—we must regard them as mystical experiences of a character that is peculiarly their own. They are contrary to the canons of ancient and modern religious art, for in these pictures our emotion surges up in a mixture of laughter and tears.

The verve which Nolde brings to sacred art beyond whose exaggerated strangeness we must look to grasp its true significance, likewise conditions his relationship to inaminate objects, still lifes, compositions and landscapes. *The Sunflowers in the Storm* (1943) and his *Seascapes* show this same destruction of form by color whose incandescence gnaws and consumes everything that is matter, destroys everything which interferes with the entry and passage of the spirit.

ERNST LUDWIG KIRCHNER

The development of Ernst Ludwig Kirchner (1880-1938), from his drawings in color of 1902 and street scenes, to which he particularly owed his fame at the time of his association with *Die Brücke*, very "Berlin" in mood, down to his final compositions which were more constructed and imbued with the *Angst* that led to his suicide, has the singularity of transforming a strictly personal feeling about form and color from within rather than in exterior manifestations. We might say that he progressed from the *Jugendstil* to Picasso towards an intellectual discipline which he hoped to develop into a kind of hieratic art. His drawings and his woodcuts, whose formal archaism seems conditioned by the very technique he employs and still more by his aim at synthesis, reflect his lively and ironic way of regarding life in general and amusing himself at the sights of the great city whose current fashions he transposes and renders almost absurd *(Five Women in a Street*, Cologne, 1913) with all the exuberance of an anecdotist or gossip writer. His later compositions are balanced in a two-dimensional structure and organization of colored surfaces which would anticipate Abstract art were it not that Kirchner preserves the figures as architectural elements. The possible influence of Matisse and Braque endow the second period of the work of Kirchner, whose imagination also inclined towards vast allegorical compositions, with an almost classical feeling, very different from that which had animated his Expressionist works.

ALFRED KUBIN

Sometimes when we rightly celebrate the fantastic draftsman, evoker of a mysterious and monstrous world, we forget Alfred Kubin (1877-1959) the painter who is truly the father of German Surrealism. He never belonged to *Die Brücke*, and, technically, we cannot put him among the Expressionists although no artist has evoked the invisible work in such apparently innocent subjects as well as he. One might think of him as a kindred spirit of Odilon Redon in the tempera paintings such as *The Days of Creation* (circa 1900) if his way of fixing the supernatural had not possessed an oddly jeering element about it which masks the horror of the visionary image that possesses him. The monsters are formed, it would seem, of the same substance as his dreams, but he exorcises them with his spirit of irony. He allows, however, an indefinable atmosphere of anguish to permeate his tempera paintings, *Sea Ghost*, *Famine* or *The Haunted Steppe* (1903-1908), all the more mysterious because the objects in them are so vague and indeterminate. That pervasive sense of mystery so frequent in the Norwegian Munch, who was one of the inspirers of Expressionism and whose woodcuts had obviously influenced Kubin, emanates from the decayed façades which hint at ghosts within, from his harassed and melancholy crowds, from normal landscapes that appear, however, overhung with fear and evil.

His authentic intimacy with the supernatural follows in the tradition of a Matthias Grünewald, a Manuel Deutsch; his captivating originality makes him at once the bridge between the fantastic painters of the fifteenth and sixteenth centuries and present-day Surrealists.

MAX BECKMANN

EDVARD MUNCH also lies perhaps behind the painting career of Max Beckmann (1884-1950), one of the most curious interpreters of the Expressionist vision of the contemporary world. His spatial conceptions arise out of a determination to transfer to the canvas all three dimensions in order to remain faithful to the reality of objects. Beckmann is one of those painters who harmonize the kind of passion for the "truth" which dominates the New Objectivity and that passion for "expression" which is absolute subjectivity. According to Expressionism, things are not what they are, they are what I feel. Beckmann's work with its emphases, sometimes exaggerated to the point of vulgarity, demands to be seen *in toto*. No shadow, no chiaroscuro, no ambiguity; if the modern world is brutal, the painting which represents it must be brutal too. Showmen and circus people and carnival masks are the favorite subjects in this society with its crude passions, exaggerated gestures, capable of refining cruelty to the point of sadism. The color is uncompromising and offers violent contrasts. War horrors and poverty dictated his "mission." "These somber faces of the dead who, from eternity, bring me their salvation, I shall paint them as such."

OSCAR KOKOSCHKA

THE major preoccupation of the Austrian painter Oscar Kokoschka (b. 1886) is not so much to contribute a new vision of the world, an unexpected expression of the visible, as to continually awake in himself and the viewer the "inner man" in portraiture, and the "interior landscape" when he is describing nature. It seems that in participating in the movement of the review *Der Sturm* which was, under the direction of the poet Herwarth Walden, a center of artistic creation almost comparable in efficiency to the *Bauhaus*, Kokoschka from the year 1910 onwards, adopted that unreality which is in fact a way of crossing over to the other side of reality in order to contemplate its "transparent face," the face that allows us to see the abyss within. Some claim to see a retarded Impressionism in his work because his Expressionism is dominated, ordered and penetrated by more subtle vibrations. He is also the creator of elemental mythologies, stripped of all the classical accessories *(The Power of Music*, Eindhoven, 1918; *The Hurricane*, Basle, 1914; *The Pagans*, 1918) in which an immense *joie de vivre* bears bodies and souls away in a frenzied orgy. He is no less visionary when he paints portraits and landscape; the model and the piece of nature, transfigured by his feverish brush in pursuit of the form in the movement it makes and unmakes, become preternatural. Every picture by Kokoschka thus presents a kind of piece of lyrical introspection, the touch turns into a plowshare and digs its furrow in the burning substance of the color that

MAX BECKMANN – PERSEUS: RIGHT-HAND WING OF TRIPTYCH. 1941 – (1,50; 0,55) FOLKWANG MUSEUM, ESSEN

is perpetually in gestation. The landscapes, apprehended in a vast impulse of pantheistic possessiveness, almost look as if their subterranean layers have been fashioned by a continuous series of earth tremors. His *Venice* (Munich, 1924), his *Mont Blanc* of the Lütjens Collection (Zurich, 1927) are manifestations of this presentiment, peculiar to our time, of an unstable world whose present form, pregnant with future forms, is merely a temporary accident.

Rolf Nesch (1893-1951), Heinrich Nauen (1880-1941) follow an aesthetic principle that is fairly close to Kokoschka's. But three Austrian painters, his compatriots, Richard Gerstl, Anton Kölig and Herbert Boeckl, pursuing their own original paths, must be mentioned particularly as presenting different aspects of this many-sided Expressionism. The somewhat rare works which we know of Richard Gerstl (1883-1908) have possibly more affinity with Corinth's tragically human anxiety, and with Munch, each of whose paintings is a question on destiny and a sentence passed on it. This young painter, who committed suicide at the age of twenty-five, enclosed in his works hints of that desperate search through forms and through human souls which finally killed him. In the personages of his pictures we see all the immobility of frozen horror. Falling for a time under the spell of Klimt, he ended by fleeing the latter's dangerous virtuosity to return to a sudden doubt about reality. A musician almost as much as a painter, a friend of Alban Berg and Schön-

OSKAR KOKOSCHKA – THE POWER OF MUSIC. 1918 – (1,02; 1,50) STEDELIJK VAN ABBE MUSEUM, EINDHOVEN

berg, to whom he gave painting lessons, he composed his pictures as if they were symphonies. This self-taught painter started painting at the age of twenty; five years later he was dead, destroyed by that *mal de vivre* which left him no respite and which even art could neither soothe nor cure.

This near-ambivalence between music and painting, mentioned in connection with Gerstl and frequent among Austrian artists, reappears in another Austrian Expressionist of the first order, Wilhelm Thöny (1888-1949). The same evil genius which cut short Gerstl's life manifested itself against the works of Thöny, about a thousand of whose paintings, constituting the major part of his production, were destroyed in 1948 in a fire in New York where he had been living since 1938. His interpretation of landscape has affinities with Kokoschka's though it lacks the dramatic power, which is replaced however by a Dufy-like poetic grace and imagination. His figures on the other hand have a mysterious gravity, a ghostlike silence, a way of appearing and disappearing as if space had condensed into substance. He lived for a time in France and his paintings of Paris, portraits of French personalities (that of Cardinal Verdier, for example) show how his initial Expressionism became transformed during his contact with an artistic ambience where other ideals prevailed.

Anton Kölig (1886-1950), the Austrian Expressionist who almost deserves to be put alongside Kokoschka, in that he possesses an analogous temperament and the latter's deep and strong dramatic feeling, is largely responsible for the revival of religious art.

Austrian too, Herbert Boeckl (b. 1894) likewise turns towards religious painting in a spirit almost as baroque as Kölig's (the churches of Maria Saal in his twentieth year and quite recently, 1959, of Seckau), but at the present moment he is branching out into an almost abstract conception of devotional art; the links of his *Saint Joseph of Cupertino* (1954) with Expressionism are very remote.

THE NEW OBJECTIVITY

THE movement which has been called the New Objectivity *(Neue Sachlichkeit)* was, at the period of its creation after 1918, a reaction against the excesses of Expressionism and aimed at a return to reality. It is however essential to grasp in its true sense the connotation which was given to the word "real"; it was not a matter of photographic naturalism or idealistic truth, but on the contrary, an art which aspired to attain the mystery that resides in the visible and wrest from it its living secret. This explains the label of "magic realism" which is sometimes applied to New Objectivity. Once more, it seems that German art is incapable of experiencing and expressing the "real" in its raw state, its immediately perceptible, everyday aspects. Even when the artists of the New Objectivity deliberately set out in search of the banal, it is almost always the fantastic that they encounter.

The New Objectivity abandons the visible for the invisible, the prosaic *terre-à-terre* for the grotesque and the tragic, and in so doing, links up with Expressionism. Among the works of Otto Dix (b. 1891), who had received an academic training and was for some time professor at Dresden Academy, are some which must be regarded as manifestos of Neo-Objective ideals, for example the *Portrait of his Parents* (Hanover, 1924). All the details are painted with the painstaking care of a "primitive"; there is no other emotion than that derived from the actual life of the subject painted. Rejection of romanticism, distaste for lyricism that idealizes things, prejudice in favor of the exclusion of the emotions of the artist, who should aim at strict objectivity—such are the characteristics in this picture which show Dix's adherence to the Neo-Realism of the twenties. But the spirit of distortion militates against the disciplines of this movement, exaggerates the wrinkled and swollen hands of this poor, hard-working couple; and this distortion is in itself an expressive and therefore Expressionistic element. In his paintings inspired by the 1914 war, *The Trench*, for example, of 1923 (this picture disappeared during the "purge" ordered under the Hitler régime), there is no more question of objective exactitude which is replaced by a prodigious accumulation of all the horrors of war in one fantastic synthesis.

Georg Grosz (b. 1893), known above all as a draftsman who, in a cold rage, stigmatized with his pencil the post-War profiteers, also transfers objective reality into something terribly unreal. Seen through the distorting mirror of anger and indignation, society and individuals reveal the monstrous idiosyncracies which everybody hides behind the mask of respectability. Grosz drew a twentieth century *Danse macabre* in which we recognize war, famine, inflation, agony, despair; and his justly most celebrated painting the *Funeral of the Poet Panizza* (Stuttgart, 1918), despite the skeleton perched on the coffin, the crowd crawling with nightmare horrors, houses collapsing as in some lunatic's dream, aims at giving an exact presentation of the torn and tottering post-1914 war world. Georg Grosz borrows certain idioms from the Futurist aesthetic—the overlapping and intersection of forms, and the systematic distortion which is the mainspring of Surrealist surprise—to take imaginary reality to its maximum expressivity. He therefore represents the extreme case of the New Objectivity which in his work is both affirmed and denied with a vehemence that defies all aesthetic systems and results in an apocalyptic conception of a universe, stripped of beauty and unworthy of redemption.

OTTO DIX – PORTRAIT OF MY PARENTS. 1924 – (1,18; 1,305) NIEDERSÄCHSISCHE LANDESGALERIE, HANOVER

Neue Sachlichkeit, interpreted literally, manifests its fidelity to the initial intentions of the movement in the paintings of Georg Schrimpf (1889-1938) who was a workman before devoting himself to painting. He thus brings to his art the mind of a manual worker, unfamiliar with the fantastic visions of a Dix or a Grosz, interested in the applied arts which he taught at Munich and, during the course of his journey to Italy, attracted by Neo-Realism whose battle organ was the review *Valori Plastici*. Schrimpf's plastic values were borrowed from the humble repertory of everyday life. His somewhat cold, mat and semi-obliterated color emphasizes the importance of volumes; his affection for the object, even when commonplace or precisely because it *is* commonplace, confers on it dignity and nobility. Xaver Fuhr (b. 1898) brings the same spirit to bear on his urban landscapes which possess an intimate and quiet grace. Self-taught, likewise, he has the lively and contrasted color, the precise drawing, the chalky tones of "Sunday painters"; he also shares their warm sympathy for the dingy slum quarters of the big city.

Wilhelm Heise has connections with this same tendency in *Neue Sachlichkeit* whereas Rudolf Schlichter belongs rather to the surrealistic branch of Grosz and Dix.

The position of Karl Hofer (1878-1955) is complex. Hofer had his "abstract" period in 1930-1931, but his main characteristic is a classicism which places him midstream between the different currents of magic realism. He had studied Cézanne in Paris and he had learned about the monumentality of simple and static figures, thus consolidating the lesson of solemn gravity which he had previously found in Hans von Marées. His pictures suffered from the persecution of so-called "degenerate" artists; several, including some of the best, were burned in spite of the fact that Karl Hofer was very much apart from the Expressionists abominated by the Nazis. His figures are calm, his nudes fixed in a refined, calculated chromatism with a smooth and warm paint quality.

DIE BLAUE REITER

No precise and formulated imperative watched over the birth of the *Blaue Reiter;* there was no manifesto stating a doctrine; the *Blaue Reiter* was more a spirit than a movement, and that is why very different artists were attracted into the group which was never explicitly an "entity" and which was above all distinguished by its eclecticism; in fact the first *Blaue Reiter* exhibition of 1911 was introduced as a kind of homage to Douanier Rousseau, and many French painters, as different from each other as Robert Delaunay and Pierre Girieud, were invited to join. This group, whose members rallied in a very flexible fashion to an aesthetic system close to that formulated by Wassili Kandinsky in *Über das Geistige in der Kunst* ("Concerning the Spiritual in Art"), published in 1912, adopted this title which was that of a review in which artists and poets also made room for musicians and Arnold Schönberg in particular. In the spirit of the *Blaue Reiter* we see a further example of that close bond between painting and music which has been such a decisive force in Romanticism; Schönberg painted, Klee played the violin. A further point:

the "Blue Horse" which gave its name both to the Review and the movement, recurs like a myth-theme in Kandinsky's and Marc's paintings, like a half-natural, half-mythical animal, almost deified, characteristic, in a word, of that Panic feeling about nature which was likewise one of the important features of the Romantic movement.

As a group the *Blaue Reiter* first defined itself as a *Sezession* from the Neue Künstlervereinigung founded by Kandinsky in 1909. Two years later, Kandinsky and Marc broke away, and in December 1911 organized the first "historic" exhibition of a collection of painters who were already playing and on the point of playing still more, as a group, a considerable rôle in European painting at the beginning of the twentieth century. According to the principles formulated by Kandinsky, forms translated into pure color should, by their expressive resonance, translate the inner resonance of things which evokes a response in the human heart. The representation of the object is entirely liberated from realist constraints which still weighed down Expressionism in general, and the artist is free to modify, overreach and even abolish them altogether following the promptings of his lyrical emotion which comes from an inner urge. Art becomes saturated with intellect in the sense that the form bursts free and is liberated from everything that could impede or warp its effusions.

The texts published in the *Blaue Reiter*, the names of the artists featuring in the two group exhibitions, prove that the intention was not to add a new "ism" to those which already existed, since it absorbed elements of Fauvism, Purism, Orphism, Cubism, Futurism, Suprematism. The ideal which exhibitors and editors of the *Blaue Reiter* shared in common was, first and foremost, absolute independence concerning what is known as the "real." It will be noticed that there is a strong proportion of Russians among the artists who are responsible for giving the aesthetics of the movement its inclination towards a warm, emotive chromatism akin to that of the French Fauves while also adding a kind of symbolic and spiritual use of color absent in the latter.

The very number and quality of the artists who figured in the *Blaue Reiter* exhibitions of 1911 and 1912 show the great amplitude acquired by this movement, whose true direction lay essentially in depth and aim, a mystique of nature flooded and transformed by the intellect. Some of these painters, distinguishable by the power of their expressive forms and the bold range of color, which they share in common with the Expressionists, nevertheless confined themselves to exterior forms; the saturation of color transfigures the substance but it is lacking in any spiritualizing effect; viewed from this angle, this what we might call, though not in any derogatory sense, the superficial branch of the *Blaue Reiter*, remained, roughly speaking, on the same plane as the Fauves. It is the case of those whom we would like to call the minor *Blaue Reiter:* Marianna von Werefkin (1870-1938), Gabriele Münter (b. 1877), Wladimir von Bechtejeff (b. 1878), Wladimir Burljuk (b. 1882), Erma Barrera-Bossi. The Expressionist aesthetic stripped of all anecdotalism, sometimes even still linked to figurative reality by a tenuous and always brittle thread, continued to predominate among the skilled and exuberant colorists whose harmonies are of an extreme boldness—Adolf Erbslöh (1881-1947), Alexander Kanoldt (1881-1939) and Alexei von Jawlensky (1864-1941). Thirteen years after the inauguration of the *Blaue Reiter*, Jawlensky was to associate himself once again with Klee, Kandinsky and Feininger to form the group, the *Blauen Vier* (the Blue Four) which is only an incident in the history of German art in the present century. Heinrich Campendonck (b. 1889) is inspired by a capricious and poetic imagination, a religious feeling that is ingenuous in its emotion, yet learned in the forms which it assumes when the artist transposes it in his stained glass windows. Alfred Kubin (1877-1959) whom we have already mentioned, much more widely known as a draftsman and book illustrator, was a prodigious explorer of the world of fantasy. The Swiss Louis-René Moilliet (1880), a friend of Klee's, with whom he traveled in Africa and of Macke's, to whom he stands in close aesthetic relationship, also belonged to the *Blaue Reiter*.

The four great personalities whose brilliant originality and strange genius set them apart from the rest of the group are August Macke, Franz Marc, Wassili Kandinsky and Paul Klee. The first two died at the Front during the 1914 War, Macke, aged twenty-seven in 1914 and Marc at thirty-six in 1916, a tragic curtailment of two fine careers whose contribution to present-day painting nevertheless remains incalculable. It was vouchsafed to Kandinsky and Klee to attain the full fruition of their genius.

AUGUST MACKE

For August Macke (1887-1914) the problem of form in space did not end, as it did in Klee and Kandinsky, with the abolition of the figure. He had not advanced either as far as Marc in whose last works the tendency towards abstract forms was becoming increasingly marked. Macke remained aloof from the fantastic and visionary elements; he deliberately remained faithful to anecdotal themes borrowed from daily life, totally void of Expressionist drama and which might seem trivial (women strolling in the street, lingering in front of shop windows, young women in a landscape), if we did not take into account the fact that the form taken from the repertory of palpable reality is merely the solution of a plastic equation. In accordance with a process analogous to that dear to La Fresnaye, and to certain periods of Delaunay and the Cubists, the colored volumes are organized in depth in an architectural construction in which the nature of the objects represented is no longer of any account. "Every form of expression in art," said Macke, "is dictated by the need to give form to ('inform') a living and vigorous emotion... Art always seizes hold of life as an entity, and the canvas is there to express it. The aim of art is not to imitate scientifically and examine the organic elements in natural forms but to produce an abbreviated form of life by means of appropriate symbols, and arouse a living emotion."

For Macke objects were no longer things living their organic life but images of things brought to another life that was simultaneously emotional and intellectual. The dissonances with which he was extremely preoccupied were intended to denaturalize the over-realistic elements, in a clump of trees for example or a dress shop window. Macke's ambition was to create another reality and confer upon it a fullness of life equal to that which objects possess in their real existence, and during the short spell of time which fate granted him he went a long way on the road towards achieving it.

AUGUST MACKE – THE DEPARTURE – (1,005; 1,305) WALLRAF-RICHARTZ-MUSEUM, COLOGNE

FRANZ MARC

PAINTER of animals without being an animal-painter, Franz Marc shared the formal preoccupations common to the artists of the *Blaue Reiter* and above all the search for a new reality through poetic unreality. If Marc progressively reduced the form of the animal to a plastic sign, it was not by virtue of an intellectual operation of the mind and reason, comparable to that which inspired French and Spanish Cubism. German and extremely romantic in character and inspiration, Franz Marc found in the animal the very essence of the forces of nature and he thought that modern man was capable of finding himself by communicating with nature through the intermediary of animals. Splendid and innocent, his favorite animals, horses—sacred among the primitive Germans—wild animals, stags and roe bucks, lead him back with them to the primal world, still unspoiled by man. "Human beings," he writes, "and above all those round about me, did not stir my real feelings; but the still virgin sense of life possessed by animals awoke in me all that was noblest. To express these elementary forms while leaving them all their powerful organic energy, is to reach the truth." Thus we should be justified in speaking about a magic realism in connection with a canvas such as the *Fate of Animals* (Basle, 1913) in which a mysterious life animates and intermingles animal and plant forms in the forest. The *Roes in the Wood*, above all in the second version, that of 1913-1914, presents an almost "non-figurative" structure, heralding the completely abstract paintings which he was to paint just before the 1914 war and the drawings he did while at the front.

This supernatural nature which he renders is always dramatic; the forest is the place of strange and terrible battles and the *Conflict of Forms* (third version,

FRANZ MARC – THE BLUE HORSES. 1911 – (1,02; 1,60) WALKER ART CENTER, MINNEAPOLIS

Munich, 1914) bears witness to a death struggle conception of the universe, the foreboding of the catastrophe which is to overtake man for having overthrown and destroyed the original harmony of creation. In Marc's art, as in his writings, we perceive a kind of Messianic passion; the urge to lead painting back to its initial and basic function, the restoration of lost harmony, of friendship between man, animals and the forest. All the work of this painter, whose generosity of heart equalled his genius, represents an immense and tragic endeavor to imbue forms that are hostile to any kind of photographic realism with the full-blooded existence unknown to those whose vision is restricted to the appearance of things. Alone in European art, for the phenomenon is frequent in the Far East, Franz Marc succeeded in becoming one with the animal, becoming animal himself, and that is why, dropping the anecdote and the accidental, he reduced it to a synthesis of rhythmic forms which are the very pulsation of life.

PAUL KLEE

THE case of Klee (1879-1940) is still more complex. Just as Marc emerged from a realism not far removed from that of the German Impressionists, Klee was a visionary from the start, even if he, too, was slightly affected by Impressionism in his earliest canvases and by the *Jugendstil.* Klee was quickly convinced that all around us exists an infinite number of potential realities, metaphysical and plastic depths, an inexhaustible diversity of visible forms in which the invisible is manifested. In order to explore the invisible world and bring away images of things which exist or could exist on other planes, the artist needs a rich and flexible enough technique to enable him, with the materials at his disposal, to interpret spontaneously the objects of his vision. Klee therefore practiced every technique, employed every material, knowing that for the particular thing in question there was only *one* means of expression, *one* material, *one* support. Just as Marc pursued the dream of universal harmony in the forms of an animal world, Klee hoped to reach right down to the very heart of creation, for in his opinion the visible world which satisfied the bulk of artists was only a tiny portion of what in fact existed. Paul Klee's ambition was always to have at hand a rich, flexible, and bold enough technique to allow him to produce an undistorted image of the invisible, rendered visible.

We have spoken of Messianism in connection with Marc; the term applies equally to Klee who formulated a theory of the mystique of the line which he taught his pupils of the *Bauhaus,*where, as an excellent teacher, he professed for some time. "The alchemy of form and color" tends to reorganize a kind of cosmic intuition which—as in Marc—strips the object of everything that is mere appearance and accident. He aims at attaining what he calls the "generating station of all space and time" in order to seize hold of the substance of the work of art so that having "left the world within, one can build in the world beyond." Disconcerting in these accents of reality which it gives to strange figures which he saw perhaps in dreams or perceived as inhabitants of "potential worlds," Klee's work is a dramatic endeavor

PAUL KLEE – STILL LIFE. 1940 – (1,00; 0,80) PAUL KLEE FOUNDATION, KUNSTMUSEUM, BERNE

to transform whatever is intuitive knowledge and visionary perception into some communicable form.

His work is not symbolic, that is the forms do not possess an immediately and clearly perceptible hieroglyphic significance. The painter's prodigious imagination, his faculty for inventing an infinitely varied plastic language, were needed to express the creatures which, in all their burning reality, truly possessed him. When we study the stages in his development and above all the transformations of his inner maturing, the ever closer adherence to the preternatural, we are able to understand the obsessive reiteration of certain figure-themes, such as the diabolical "angels" of his last years, the choice, on occasion, of crude materials, rough and torn canvases, pictures constructed on the principle of musical fugues, imaginary cities that seem constructed of spiders' webs, gardens teeming with unreal but convincing vegetation. If Klee's most fantastic works give us an impression of absolute truth, it is because their reality is situated in a domain where he alone could penetrate and he walked as the lord and master. "Now the objects perceive me," he used to say, when he was satisfied with a picture.

For Klee the function of art is to find a means of expressing the secret order of the fabric of life which is equally valid "for animals, plants, human beings, earth,

PAUL KLEE – LA BELLE JARDINIÈRE. 1939 – (0,96; 0,71) PAUL KLEE FOUNDATION, KUNSTMUSEUM, BERNE

PAUL KLEE – MAIN ROAD AND SECONDARY ROAD. 1929 – (0,83; 0,67)
PRIVATE COLLECTION, COLOGNE

air, fire, water and even, at the same time, for all the forces which gravitate round the center." We might well believe that to write as Klee does, "it is with God alone that I seek a place for myself" and to define himself as a cosmic *point d'appui* is to stray beyond the realm of art into that of the mystical and metaphysical, but this same conception of the sacred function of art is also Marc's; it is as valid for these modern painters as it was for the Romantics and the artists of the Middle ages.

Klee showed that the "real" vastly overflows the common, visible world. Musician, architect, mathematician, perhaps even biologist, he observed that the universe obeyed not the precepts of human reason, which has often turned its back on the real, but rather the inner logic of things. Georg Schmidt claims that he was the greatest realist of our time, the artist richest in human experience and creative power. Realizing that when he looked at the exterior form of objects, he was only seeing a poor substitute, Klee situated himself in the very heart of things, in the same way that Marc transformed himself into a horse or a roe buck. This aptitude for the visionary in Klee is bound up with his affection and solicitude for his craft. During his time at the *Bauhaus* he took an active interest in the various techniques practiced there—ceramics, weaving, wrought-iron, for he was always searching for new media capable of embracing still more closely the reality he was so eager to make manifest. No painter of our time has shown himself so enterprising in his manner of painting and given evidence of so sure a touch in his innovations, as if the fact of aspiring to artisan perfection offered a further possibility of penetrating more deeply into the very substance of things.

WASSILI KANDINSKY

There is no question of annexing Wassili Kandinsky (1866-1944) to German painting, but this account would be incomplete if we did not make room for an artist whose work and influence count among the fundamental elements of contemporary art. This Russian, with Mongol blood in his veins, born in Moscow, who divided his life between his native country, Germany and France (where he lived his last years and where he died) is the inspiration behind the most important movements of Post-Expressionist German painting. In 1902 he created the group known as the "Phalanx"; then he founded the *Neue Künstlervereinigung* and the *Blauen Vier;* his teaching at the *Bauhaus*, finally, is one of the great realizations of that institution. By his example and passionate research after a form that becomes a pure spiritual movement with access to cosmic nature, and his rejection of the figurative representation of nature's exterior aspects in order the better to comprehend its great undercurrents, Kandinsky rises before us as one of the pillars of modern art in Germany as well as in Russia and France. His book *Concerning the Spiritual in Art (Über das Geistige in der Kunst)* and Worringer's *Abstraktion und Einfühling*, which appeared at the same period, are the great basic texts in which the principles and justifications of a non-figurative art are set forth.

To the "German period" belong first and foremost Kandinsky's paintings of circa 1910-1912, in which the landscape elements lose their physical definition and are transformed into rhythms. In the gallop of the blue horseman riding across these landscapes, currents and dynamisms are set up which no longer aim at representing such things but at being their own essence. Liberated from every reference to the naturalist vocabulary of objects, his creative emotion, completely independent, finds an outlet in the invention of forms and colors—the "dramatic period" succeeding that of the *Blaue Reiter*. Then in the so-called "architectural period" he demonstrates the potentiality of non-figurativism as a vehicle for conveying direct and undiluted feeling. Kandinsky's partly romantic, partly constructive temperament, once the artist had jettisoned those objects which, he said, "interfered with his painting," opened up a wider and in fact boundless field.

Kandinsky was not only the author and publisher of the review, the *Blaue Reiter*, which gathered round it the liveliest and most original forces in German art in 1911-1912, but also, and this especially, the soul of the group, which he supplied with a doctrine, spirit and unity. The 1914 war temporarily interrupted his active participation in the evolution of German painting since he did not return there until 1921 after a prolonged stay in Russia. It is not difficult to recognize in contemporary abstract art, as a kind of legacy of the *Blaue Reiter* movement, the triple contribution of Marc, Klee and Kandinsky; on this score, the latter could hardly be excluded from this lineage, whose greatness he did so much to advance.

THE BAUHAUS

THE *Bauhaus*, which was founded in Weimar in 1919 and subsequently migrated to Dessau and finally came to an end with the advent of National Socialism in 1933, is the creation of the architect Walter Gropius. His principal aims were to get artists and craftsmen, who shared the same ideals, to work together in the same ambience, to re-establish the feeling of functionalism, of the dignity and beauty of the every day object in the realm of architecture and the decorative arts, to restore harmony between man and the setting in which he lives, to ennoble industry by urging the production of beautiful as well as practical shapes. "The widespread notion that art is a luxury is the disastrous consequence of the spirit of yesterday which isolated phenomena ("art for art's sake") and, in this way, divorced them from collective life."[24] For the old academies and art schools the *Bauhaus* substituted studios in which workmen and artists worked side by side and taught each other; what the artists learned in contact with the craftsmen has often been recalled by Kandinsky and Klee who were teachers at the *Bauhaus*.

This aesthetic and still more social ideal is near enough to that which inspired the Constructivists and Suprematists in Russia and which one finds frequently set out in Holland in the articles which Mondrian and Van Doesburg wrote in the review *De Stijl*. The story of the *Bauhaus* belongs chiefly to the story of the evolution of the decorative arts in Germany, and it is significant that the founder was an architect.

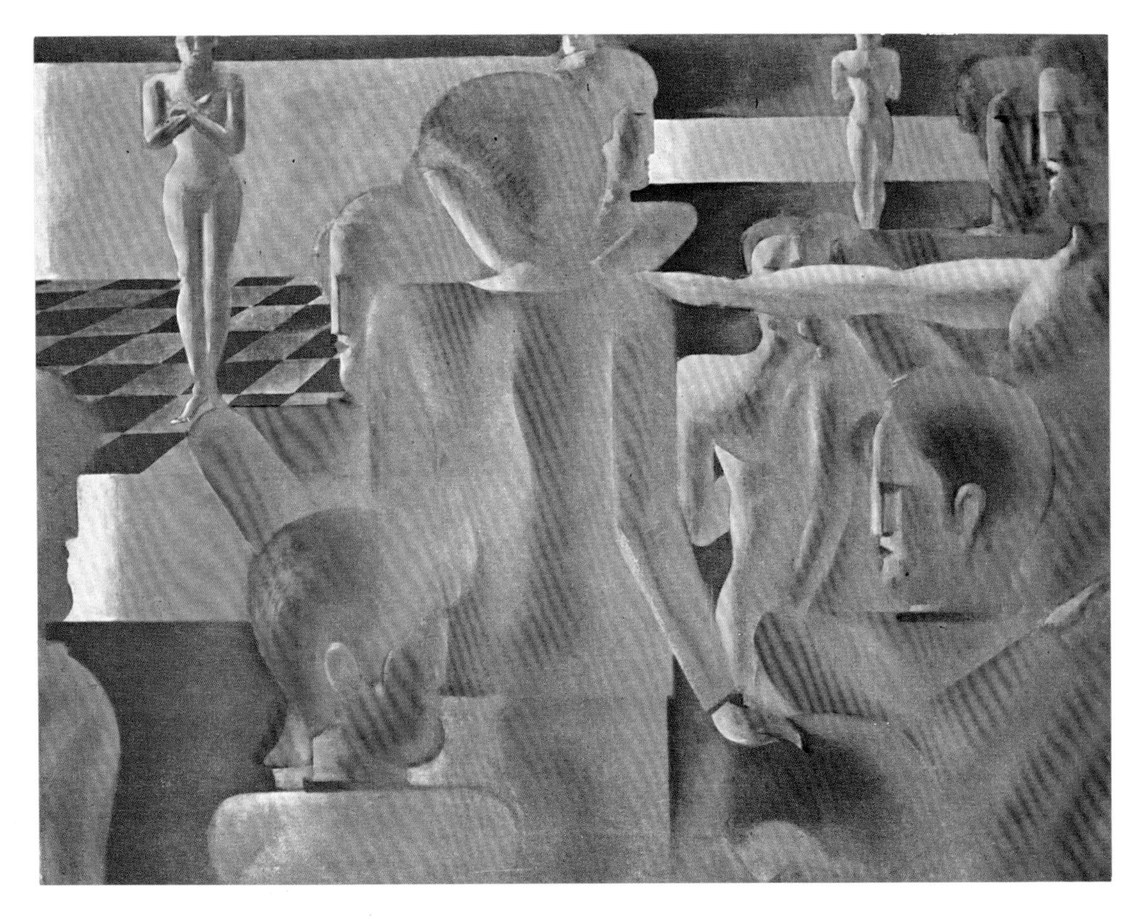

OSKAR SCHLEMMER – FOURTEEN PERSONS IN AN IMAGINARY SETTING. 1930 – (0,915; 1,205) WALLRAF-RICHARTZ-MUSEUM, COLOGNE

But the part allotted to painting and the training which a great number of painters—H. Bayer, F. Schleifer, M. Breuer, Hirschfeld-Mack, W. Herzger, P. Citroen, G. Muche, J. Itten—obtained there, the far from negligible orientation which the painters who taught there received—Moholy-Nagy, Oscar Schlemmer, Lyonel Feininger, Josef Albers, Kandinsky and Klee themselves—oblige us to consider the heroic experiment of the *Bauhaus* as one of the extremely vital moments in the evolution of German painting during the period extending from the end of the First World War to the outbreak of the Second. The fact that the *Bauhaus* was also concerned with the theater, dancing and the cinema considerably widened the experimental field of both teachers and pupils.

The reintegration of the painter into city life, his removal from his ivory tower, the invitation to exchange his solitude for continual daily contact with other

rative but which could with more justification be called co
minates everything which is not form itself. Figurative or no
Bauhaus belong implicitly or explicitly to a kind of communit
imagine Kirchner or Beckmann participating. For it was
ate in the *Bauhaus* without having, at least partially, imbib
ic sense of vocation characteristic of that non-religious Order,
ost religious ideal. For it was not only a matter of an aestheti
al reconstruction in line with principles comparable to those on wh
de to found a new society or a new humanity.

Lyonel Feininger (b. 1871), at the same time as Marcks and Itten
t painters invited to teach and work at the *Bauhaus*. Feininge
style in landscape in which the study he had made of Cubism an
ad held his interest for some time, resulted in a certain geometrizati
s entirely original contribution is light. When he painted *Halle*
is one of his favorite subjects, or that of Soest, the paint is split up in
which reconstruct the form and suggest the imponderability of an
parent paint-substance. Very subtle and of a calculated refineme
dral, 1930 or the *Barfüsser-Kirche* in Erfurt, 1927), his painting creat
stic edifices which partake of the nature of mirages. In its appli
ican buildings and factories, after the artist's period of residence in th
ulted in a new beauty that was both real and poetic. The contribu
m find in him an outlet denied them elsewhere. Feininger restores t
hat virtue which it possesses of absorbing and re-creating luminosity
s nothing but a thing wholly composed of light.

Two years after Feininger, who had joined in 1919, Oscar Schlemm
), was invited in his turn. The multiplicity of this artist's talents, wh
ded exactly to the ideal of universality which was the *Bauhaus* cree
ompose theatrical diversions for which he designed sets and costu
the origin of the famous *Ballet Triadique*—in which near-abstract fig
t—that still remains a date in the history of the contemporary
red spirit of the Constructivists, Schlemmer sought out a crystalizati
ilized in a simplification of almost motionless volumes which deter
movements in space by virtue of their position alone and the mere s
ible movements. A strange peace emanates from this world of
which personages, like statues hewn in great rudimentary walls, in
re everything is purity, tranquillity, calm radiation of intelligence, f
a changeless perpetuity.

The formal austerity which was the rule in this School, equa
m the emotional or sensual outpourings of Expressionism and
ddle class art, attracted the artists who aspired to this "Reform
ich Gropius had introduced. Nothing could be more absurd th

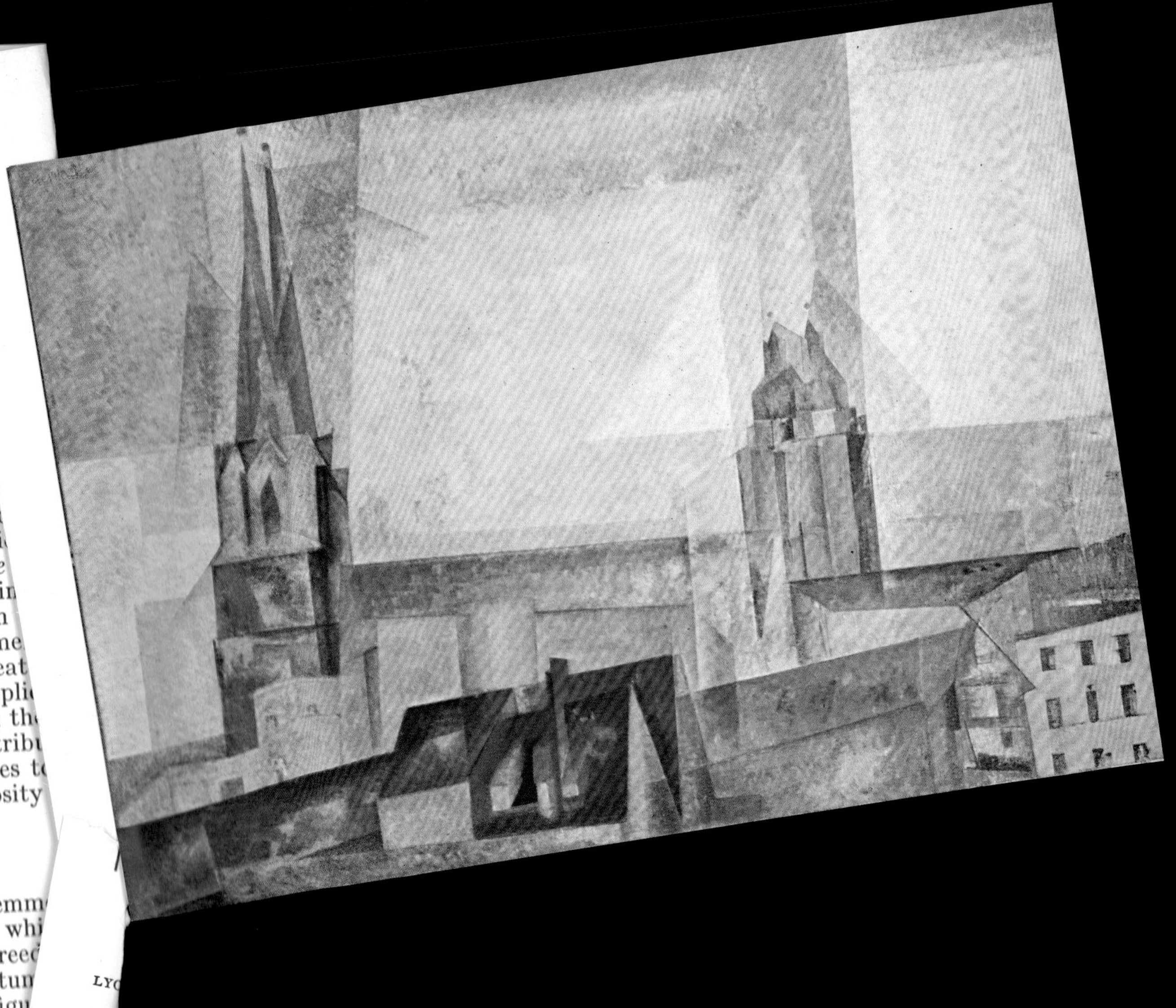

LYO

peo
cert
lack
in al
tutio

from
form
of vo
tectu
eleme
was b

cannot
collabo
Messia
an alm
of a to
are m

the fi
grand
that h
but h
which
light
transp
Cathe
fanta
Amer
it re
Cubi
art t
seem

1943
spon
to c
was

WALLRAF-RIC

the Nazis leveled against the *Bauhaus* of being a "breeding-ground of Bolshevist culture"; on the contrary, what was set up there was a new form of classicism, founded on severity.

Josef Albers (b. 1888) whose art is strictly geometrical and is still further marked by a veritable asceticism of color (white and black, or chromatic experiments of extreme subtlety) adopts a constructivist functionalism which he has never deserted.

The place assigned to the applied arts and industrial design led the *Bauhaus* towards ideals and imperatives comparable to those set forth by Mondrian and Van Doesburg in *De Stijl* and brought it close to the experiments of Malewitch, Pevsner, Tatlin, Gabo, and Lissitzky; and it was a Hungarian, Laszlo Moholy-Nagy (1895-1946) who in an infinite variety of works from architecture to photographic montage, determined the totalitarianism of the *Bauhaus*, and who took up Gropius' initial idea, transplanted it in America after National Socialism had dissolved that organization and founded the *New Bauhaus* in Chicago.

Endowed with an insatiable curiosity which was always urging him forward to new experiments, Moholy-Nagy is probably destined to remain more famous for those interesting and fertile experiments than for his work as a painter in the strict sense—which hardly does him full justice.

THE MERZBAU: KURT SCHWITTERS

To understand the significance and importance of the work of Kurt Schwitters (1887-1948), we must consider simultaneously the vital part he played in the birth of the *Dada* movement at Zurich in 1917 which, negative and destructive, was fertile precisely in making a clean sweep of all the old values and the constructive element in his work, the *Merzbau*. In all destruction there is a certain leaven and the announcement of a new creation. Schwitters can be said to have pursued his individual *Dada* movement in Hanover where he lived up to 1933, composing collages in which the refinement of the form and color, combining with the strangeness of the material, plus the surprise factor of the unusual, attained a vigor and at the same time a grace of an entirely personal nature. This collage technique, which was destined to have an extensive influence, and only too often became a kind of game, was seriously practiced by Kurt Schwitters with the nicety and assumed primitiveness of the skilled miniaturist. The metro ticket, tobacco packet, theater ticket, which became banalities after him, had at that time all their surprising novelty.

From this fortuitous two-dimensional arrangement of surfaces, borrowed from a wide variety of materials, Kurt Schwitters passed quite naturally to three-dimensional construction in which surfaces were replaced by volumes and in which the oddest substances were to find a place, for which he invented the term *Merzbau* or, Merz-Construction. In *Merzism* Schwitters saw himself as the constructor of a purely gratuitous architecture without function or finality which presented itself as a kind of collage in space. The *Merz* was to be an object, in the interior of which the viewer took his place to contemplate it and which acted on him in the way atmosphere does. The spectator was inclined to regard *Merzbau* as an eccentric game of intriguing originality, but for Schwitters himself it was "a cathedral," that is to say a sacred edifice. The *Merz* which he constructed thus, first in Germany then in the U.S.A. to which he had emigrated, no longer exists, and it is impossible—except through the medium of photographs—to gain a proper idea of what Schwitters notion was. This "monument constructed by things in homage to their own silence," seemed a piece of bric-à-brac to those who failed to divine its message, but it corresponded to a real spirit of *Angst*. Beckmann, on seeing the first Merz-Construction—the example in Hanover—was almost frightened when confronted with "this infinite space, the foreground of which would need to be ceaselessly filled with any bric-à-brac to hide its terrifying depth from view."

The magic object, possessed of an incantatory force, all the more powerful because it exploited the shock caused by the unusual and fantastic, which assumed a completely autonomous life for the Dadaists and for the Surrealists the supernatural virtue of bewitched banality, made its entry into the *Merzbau* with a shock-value, independent of any symbolism. Its presence alone, the mere fact of existing, raised it to the height of a magic spell. The challenges of chance, the rich fecundity of strange encounters, the secret energy of the incongruous—mainsprings of Dadaism and Surrealism—were in Schwitters allied to a religious conception of the Merz-Cathedral.

SURREALISM

IN Germany, as in other countries, the mainsprings of Surrealism consist of a paradoxical apprehension of visible reality, in a strange association of objects whose relationships to each other are presented in an astonishing and sometimes a shocking novelty. With the Surrealists we find the almost unconscious abandonment to the purely fantastic, and also the employment of unlimited sources of amazement, stupor, sensory or intellectual shock. The initiators of the *Dada* movement, Kurt Schwitters and Max Ernst can be regarded as the masters of present-day Surrealism. The latter, who is German by birth but appears under the banner of the School of Paris, will not be dealt with here for that reason, although his art has deeply buried roots in the fertile land of the fantastic painters of the fifteenth and sixteenth centuries, his real ancestors.

Rarely does the fantastic exist in its pure state; it is more often manifested by the way in which it organizes novel combinations of the objects or fragments of things of daily life which acquire, by virtue of these unexpected associations, a strange significance and the glamor of novelty. In order to explain the singularities in the paintings of Simon van Keulen (b. 1926), Joachim Lüdke (b. 1925), Rol Richter (b. 1927) and Leo Cremer (b. 1911), we should need to return to the theory of *meraviglia*, that is the surprising as a creative principle, which likewise underlies the Baroque and is taken by the Surrealists to *reductio ad absurdum.* Reconstructing the universe according to the whims of one's personal imagination, one's visionary capacity for laying hold of the invisible and from them constructing an unprecedented universe, is a technique common to painters like Heinrich von Hessen, Fabius von Gugel, Bele Bachem, Rudolf Hausner, Paul Meissner, Heinz Rose. The technique of collage, which with Max Ernst had become a means of expression of obsessive intensity, can be considered the perfect summing-up of Surrealist methods.

The style of these fantastic modern painters does not differ essentially from the French and Italian styles. Leo Cremer comes close to Clerici, Rose has an affinity with Chirico; but, more personal because more instinctive, Werner Gilles (b. 1894) and Heinz Trökes (b. 1913) are situated on the border of the fantastic and of Abstraction because their figures are deliberate inventions, independent of prototypes which already exist in nature and at the same time sufficiently denaturalized to avoid any hint of relationship with normal objectivity. Whereas Gilles pursues a poetic reverie which materializes into subtle colors, Trökes imagines and realizes the substances of a possible world, credible, though existing only in his own fantasy. To this world his vigorous imagination and his faculty for giving substance to what was only a dream lend a curious solidity. Perhaps in their desperation to survey all the potentialities of the things that lie beyond sensory perception, these painters are spiritual heirs of Paul Klee.

Edgar Ende (b. 1901), Mac Zimmermann (b. 1912) are content rather to make use of a distorting inspiration to transform common elements. It would be possible to demonstrate analogies between the styles of Zimmermann and Dali—the minutiae, the almost miniaturist painstaking quality of certain portions of the picture contrasting with the striking incongruity of their association, suggesting a lunatic world in which matter itself has lost its reason. Ende, on the contrary, imbued with a melancholy and dreamy poetry, describes a world of desolation after a great cataclysm has swept over it.

Apocalyptic too is the world of the Austrian Ernst Fuchs (b. 1930) who with all the patience of the old masters, paints the miracles of alchemy and terrors of the Last Judgment. For Alfred Kremer (b. 1895) salvation presents itself in the form of a spoliation, a return to the symbol, the hieroglyph containing the secret life of the human being, and this would appear to connect him with Abstraction rather than with Surrealism in the accepted sense.

ABSTRACT ART

THE development of the feeling of form which was produced on the one hand in the drawing of the *Jugendstil* and related "unrealist" movements and, on the other, in the dramatic and violent style of Expressionism (Georg Kaiser: "We live from explosion to explosion"), resulted in a state of rupture and dislocation of that form. French Cubism and Fauvism, Russian Suprematism and Constructivism, the Neo-plasticism of the Dutch, Italian Futurism, also affected, from outside, that formal anxiety in its search for new ways. The plastic asceticism of the *Bauhaus*, the pursuit of a "spiritual" element, limited and constrained by traditional (i.e. figurative) form, among the *Blaue Reiter* painters, oriented this research towards representational idioms in which the form directly expressed the emotion without recourse to the vocabulary of natural objects. Abstract art makes its appearance as a normal and obvious consequence of what was happening within the *Blaue Reiter*, especially in Franz Marc and Wassili Kandinsky; the former was prevented by his early death from reaching this non-figurative art whose birth is anticipated in his last works; as for Kandinsky, in the period which runs from his first abstract compositions of 1910 to his death in 1944, he covers the whole range of pictorial and plastic possibilities of an art wholly independent of the representation of nature.

Two main tendencies, contingent on the quality of the necessity which drove the artist to reject naturalistic forms, separate the abstract painters into those who pursue the denudation of creative emotion at the expense of strict objectivity and the "lyricists" who advocate and adopt non-figuration because of the possibility it offers of translating a state of consciousness, an impulse of passion immediately and directly into the spontaneous efflorescence of forms and colors, governed less by the intellect (as with the geometricians) than the promptings of intuition and exuberance. These two different currents are exemplified in German painting by Josef Albers (b. 1888) on the one hand, and on the other the Czech Franz Kupka (1871-1956) or the German Otto Freundlich (1909-1943).

A professor at the *Bauhaus*, Josef Albers practiced with an outstanding economy of expression an art of essential purity, based on harmony of proportions, and the suggestive virtue of numbers. His geometric forms strive towards a total occupation of space, not through the utilization of perspective or illusionist devices, but a skilful arrangement of planes to create the said space, whereas the majority of painters—especially "figurative"—are mostly content to suggest it. The ascetic severity of this art is one of the most moving examples of what geometric non-figuration produces when guided by a high intelligence allied to the most refined sensibility.

Whether he is stirring great colored waves or setting up grave yet simple architecture, Kupka had regained something of the graphism of the *Jugendstil*, and in certain of his works he can be compared to Schmithals himself; but this is not the distinctive mark of his personality. An instinctive artist, passionately fond of opulent colors, he composes chromatic fireworks which resound with a vigorous *joie de vivre.*

Otto Freundlich, more introspective, more anxious, looked for a social message and almost a Messianic communion in artistic creation. A solemn and pure figure, candid and upright, Freundlich retained a concern for the form, gathered on itself, plastic equilibrium, even in those of his pictures in which the emotion is most intense and naked.

Geometric abstraction is not so natural to the German temperament—always more romantic than classical—as the lyricism of effusion, organic exuberance. Friedrich Vordemberg-Gildewart (b. 1899) arranges geometric figures with a severe and somewhat cold grace in relationships of great intellectual finesse, and among the painters of a younger generation we also encounter some "geometrics" like Heinrich Siepmann, and occasionally Georg Meistermann (b. 1911) who is, in addition, a stained-glass artist and who translates his religious emotion sometimes in stable constructions which express the tranquillity of rational reasoning, at others the conflict of forms and clashes of color which are transcriptions of a soul fraught with anxiety.

The position of Willi Baumeister (1889-1956) in the Abstract art of contemporary Germany is characterized by a mythological feeling that controls the forms and at the same time constitutes a repertory of emotional signs, hieroglyphs endowed with a strange intimate vitality and an expression of elemental forces by which he allows himself to be guided. "Personal symbolic language" (Grohmann), but above all, inventions of images which are not the representation of a reality received by man's normal perceptions nor a rational construction of the intellect, but the recording of a waking dream, the forms of Baumeister have a complete plastic liberty; yet they could just as well be regarded as ideograms. After going through the Expressionistic experiment, and trying out Cubism, Baumeister invented a language as capable of rendering the fantasies of his unconscious mind—in which he comes close to the Surrealists—as the intuitive perception of the organic thrust which stirs the universe. The wealth and variety of the materials employed, the impasto evoking a tactile sensation, the incorporation of sand with oil paint, serve to translate directly strange inspirations which traditional processes could only render imperfectly.

Hieroglyphs that show a more interiorized spirit than Baumeister's are the distinctive components of the pictures of Julius Bissier (b. 1893). This painter was one of the founders of the *Zen* movement which in 1949 collected round it a number of artists eager to contribute a powerful spiritual content to Abstract form and who wished to indicate by the analogy of their title with Buddhist Zen that they obey the principles of a mystic naturalism, heedful to the voice of the soul of things.

For Karl Otto Goetz (b. 1914) the characteristic is not so much a résumé of an intellectual and mystical experience as the projection of a magic state which is not immured in its own passion, and opens, on the contrary, into lines of force which have an inherent sense of tragedy and whose violent waves are recorded by the artist. An extremely discreet use of color—with a preference for black and white—reinforces this expression of primordial energy whose field of action is the work of art, and the painter the half-conscious interpreter. Its form is its linear sign, but it is, above all, movement, dynamic creation which its own exuberance carries into space and fills that space with currents of energy in which the paintings collect like stars in the Milky Way. In these works, as in those of Emil Schumacher (b. 1912), K.R.H. Sondenborg (b. 1923) and Wilhelm Wessel (1904), a perpetually changing universe sets its

WILLI BAUMEISTER – WALL-PAINTING. 1923 – (1,175; 0,685) MARGARETE BAUMEISTER COLLECTION, STUTTGART

whirlwinds in motion, and we are reminded of the convulsions of a primordial world agitated by the tremors of the first metamorphoses.

This way of surprising and representing nature, no longer in its limited and fixed characteristics, but in its great cosmic pulsations, indicates among the various contemporary tendencies of Abstract art the one which corresponds most closely to the thought and feeling of German artists from the Danube School and Romantics to the present day.

Fritz Winter (b. 1905) has composed among other works a series of gouaches which he entitles forces or elemental earth-impulses, in which we seem to catch the subterranean forces which fashion the mineral world at their mysterious task. The painter "leaves the model of the visible to penetrate into realms of a new mobility; he thus gives visible forms to experiences inaccessible to figurative painting—the life-urge, the deep forces of the earth, plant-life, breaths and currents." (Haftmann)

As opposed to the young School of Hamburg (Strombeerger, Mahlmann, Breest) who were searching for a common ground between Constructivism and Neo-Plasticism, the painters of the *Zen* group, the *Junge Westen*, allowed themselves to be guided by a cosmic intuition urging them to seize the very essence of life in its primordial transmutations. It is in this light that we should regard the pictures of Hans Trier (b. 1915), Emil Schumacher (b. 1912) Bernhard Schultze (b.1915), which represent bold and impassioned attempts to wrest from chaos—the principle of a disordered nature—structures on which a kind of wild harmony can be established of which the artist will be merely the recording apparatus, the seismographer.

The danger threatening this means of plastic expression may well be the risk of slipping into formlessness, the desire to escape the constraints of an intellectually constructed form; in an extreme case, going so far as to refuse every form as such, with the creative act claiming to keep the instinctive spontaneity of a cry intact. For German artists particularly, always inclined to be suspicious of tyrannical self-limitation in severe formal disciplines, it constitutes a major temptation. A painter like Wols, German by birth, who normally appears among the artists of the so-called School of Paris, has taken this aspiration towards the "informal" to its ultimate extreme. But this virtual informalism can and must, by the very fact of becoming expression, become form at the same time. The crux of the problem lies in the pictorial instinct and formative will, in their accord and harmony. From this point of view, the works of Ernst Wilhelm Nay (b. 1902) which possess their own "order" without any sacrifice of freshness or spontaneity, are characteristic of an aesthetic which approaches that of music.

Such too is the work of Th. Werner (b. 1886) who was one of the promoters of the *Zen* group and in 1949 laid down as the guiding principle of the ideals of that movement the fusion of the individual world of the artist with the universal forces which surround and penetrate him, in and through the picture. While refusing to yield to a metaphysical aim—"pictures are not made with ideas or objects but with color" he said—he allows himself to be impregnated with that *cosmic realism* which reaches out beyond perceptible reality because human perception can contact only the fringes and the most superficial epidermis of the world we live in.

THE vitality of German painting, so striking, as we have just seen, in the twentieth century, is characterized by the rare continuity of almost seven centuries; a record with few equivalents outside the French and Italian Schools. The very abundance of artists makes us acutely aware of the limits imposed on this study, since we have been obliged to neglect a great number of anonymous masters of the fifteenth and sixteenth centuries and also omit in more recent times too many artists, of the second rank, perhaps, but nevertheless far from negligible. With insufficient space to provide an adequate analysis of their contributions, we should run the risk of producing a list of names as dry as a catalogue.

German painting is altogether remarkable in the homogeneity of its inspiration. We have noted the main features—its consistent fidelity to nature, which sustains even the strangest works; and, above all, from its origins to the very latest experiments and through the most varied aesthetic forms, a persistent sense of anxiety.

It would certainly seem that it is this *Angst*, which, piercing through a certain bravura and exaggeration in the paintings of the Primitives and continuing through the Baroque and Romantic periods, asserts itself as the great "constant" in the German painter. If he prefers to neglect the laws of a French type of classicism lest they should impose their static qualities on him, he never fails to find his natural idiom and basic principle in some form of expressionism.

NOTES

1 – His work is to be seen in the great *Crucifixion* in the church of Sankt Maria zur Höhen, Soest (c. 1480), in the altarpiece of the parish church of Schöppingen (c. 1460-1470) and in the museum at Münster. The Master of Liesborn, like his successor and disciple, the Master of Cappenberg, who was working in Münster between 1510 and 1530, submitted to the aesthetic principles of Cologne, and his agreable eclecticism successfully reconciles the characters of the two schools.

2 – The author of the *Crucifixion of Svx. Barbora* (Prague, pre-1400), of the Hluboka *Adoration of the Shepherds*, (Hluboka Castle, pre-1400) and of the Crucifixion of Hohenfurth (Prague, c. 1400), which possesses a grave and serene beauty with its gradations of brown that stand out against a gold background; and finally, the interesting author of the Altarpiece of Dubecek (Prague, c. 1400), which is of truly royal distinction though not without a touch of mannerism.

It is this mannerism which, following the grand style of the Master of Wittingau and the realism of Master Theodoric, was to inspire a profusion of altarpieces, amongst them the *Altar of St. James*, painted about 1440, originating from Brno, the thirteen panels of which are now dispersed among seven museums and private collections in Central Europe, which makes it difficult to study them; the *Epitaph* by Jan Jeren (c. 1395), shared between Prague and Vienna; the *Altar of Hyrov* (Prague, c. 1430); the Altar of Namest (Provincial Museum, Brno, c. 1430).

One of the most attractive ensembles of the art of the first half of the fifteenth century, belonging to the "grand style" and in the Byzantine tradition, is the cycle of the church of the Capucins, Prague, painted before 1410 — and now in the National Gallery there. The heads of the figures, in which monotony is avoided only through the variety of headdress and style of beard, possess an intensity of expression, certainly less marked than in Master Theodoric's work, yet striking enough, and heightened moreover by the almost camaïeu tone in which golden browns predominate.

3 – Between the *Madonna of Most* (Capucin monastery, Most, pre-1350) which has an element of Cimabue, and the *Assunta de Lanna* (Prague) which dates from 1450, we have, in the course of a century, a series of every possible type of beauty: the graceful and almost paganly handsome Madonnas of the Master of the cycle of Hohenfurth (Prague, 1350), the *Madonna of Strahov* and the *Madonna of Veveri* (both Prague, 1350). Some anecdotal details, picturesque and charming — the throne transformed into a fairy palace with chirruping angels — in the *Madonna of Kladsko* (Berlin, c. 1350), the somewhat heavy but moving realism of the *Madonna of Zbraslav* (parish church, Zbraslav, c. 1360) and the exquisite grace of the so-called *Madonna of Rome* (Prague, c. 1360), perhaps the best example of the "soft style" of the second half of the fourteenth century, show the great variety of spirit to be found in Czech painting of this period.

4 – The most characteristic paintings of this flourishing and profane style are the *Madonna of St. Vitus* (Prague, c. 1400), the *Madonna of Lnare* (Conventual Church of the Holy Trinity, Lnare, post 1400) and the *Madonna of Slara Koruna* (Prague, c. 1410).

5 – He was born about 1400, at Bruneck in the Tyrol, and it seems likely that it was with the painter known as the Master of Uttenheim that he acquired the rudiments of a robust and frank art, open to Italian influences which penetrated into Nordic countries, quite naturally following the routes through the Tyrolean valleys, which thus became a fruitful scene of exchanges between the journeymen artists of the Latin countries and those of the Germanic countries. The sober, massive and stocky grandeur to be observed in the altarpieces which the Master of Uttenheim painted for the church in Neustift and which represent episodes in the *Life of St. Augustine* (in the Neustift Gallery and in Munich; probably painted in 1453) did not depart from the Tyrolean tradition. On the contrary, when we study the *Altarpiece of*

St. Catherine in the same Neustift Gallery, painted by Friedrich Pacher in 1463, we find, in the combination of the embossed gold backgrounds and foreshortenings reminiscent of Mantegna and Paolo Uccello, an evident desire to continue the new discoveries of the Renaissance with traditional elements. Friedrich Pacher's work is not wholly free from clumsiness and his pictorial mastery is not the ideal instrument for the capricious imagination which inspired, for example, the *Baptism of Christ* of the Freising Klerikalseminar (1483) in which we see the earth strewn with Crivelli-like fruits with birds hopping solemnly among them, while the Gothic bell-turrets of the background incline together with a delightful suppleness to form a canopy above the Redeemer's head.

6 – Jan Pollack, who, to judge by his name, was probably of Polish origin, and whom we find established in Munich in 1484 where he died in 1519, was probably familiar with certain works of Michael Pacher and thought about the latter's aesthetic ideas, but it is particularly in Austria itself, in the Master of Gross-Gmain, who broke away from Frueauf in order to join the Tyrolean (he was living in Salzburg between 1480 and 1500), in Urban Goesrtschader (working in Villach between 1511 and 1530), a little known Carinthian, but very original in form and spirit, and finally in the Master of St. Korbinian, who actually modelled himself more on Friedrich Pacher's style, that the extent and variety of the Pacher contribution is to be seen.

7 – Dürer is too much of a cosmopolitan, not to say intellectual, to surrender more than the smallest part of himself to the fantastic. But, though less evident, less sumptuosly displayed than in Grünewald, Baldung or the Lansquenets, this penchant for the supernatural, this feeling for the fantastic is nevertheless brought out by the terror caused him by a dream he had one night about the end of the world and the transcribed and painted version he made of it on waking.

8 – This is so true that the Faustian portrait, the portrait of the "potential essence", assumes, as we shall see later, a considerable place in sixteenth century art and persists uninterruptedly through Romanticism into Expressionism. Amongst the painters of the seventeenth and eighteenth centuries we rediscover this tradition of the Faustian portrait in *The Widow* by Daniel Preissler (1666-1737) in Berlin, Moritz Kellerhoven's *Self-Portrait* among the Romantics, *We Three* by Philipp Otto Runge (1805, burned in 1932), the admirable drawing by Friedrich showing him with the haunted look of a man dogged by madness, *The Portrait of Lucas* by Fohr (1795-1818), (Heidelberg, 1816), Janssen's *Self Portrait* (Hamburg, 1807-1845), and, nearer our own time, the *Self Portrait* by Lovis Corinth (Cologne, 1858-1925) and the tragic one by Kokoschka (1886) as a "Degenerate artist" — an allusion to the destruction by the Nazis of what they considered "degenerate art".

9 – It would require a long discussion to attempt to elucidate what is known as the "Grünewald problem", raised some thirty years ago by erudite scholars dissatisfied with Sandrart's affirmations, accepted by tradition. The studies by Hans Gröniger, A. Bürkhard, Hans Heinrich Naumann, Hans Haug and above all W.K. Zülch have raised the question of the identity of the author of the Isenheim altarpiece and of the artist known under the name of Matthias Grünewald; they claim to have discovered this author in painters whose biography remains little known; Mathis Nithard and Mathis Gothardt have been mentioned. Zülch considers the painter of the Antonites to be a certain Mathis Gothard Nithardt who died in Halle in 1528 after being involved in a tragic manner in the Peasants' War.

10 – With Cardinal Uriel von Gemmingen, Archbishop of Mainz, and Cardinal Albrecht von Brandenburg.

11 – One also associates with his name, because of the great similarities, possibly even borrowings, to be found in his Altarpiece of Herrenberg (Stuttgart), the strange Jörg Ratgeb of Gmund (c. 1480-1526), of whom comparatively little is known, save that he died — as perhaps Grünewald did — in the Peasants' War. Ratgeb is a visionary of the same "family" as Grünewald, and like him, in love, if more naïvely and clumsily, with the *magic realism* which transfigures things in this world.

It is on the other hand difficult to discover a direct relationship between the Master of Isenheim and a very strange

Bavarian painter, Gabriel Mälesskircher (c. 1430-1495). Mälesskircher is a man of the fifteenth century, but, more modern than his contemporaries, he has less affinity with them than with artists of the sixteenth century. His Munich *Crucifixion* is a Baroque masterpiece, quite unusual at this period and revealing in its author a temperament inclined towards the exaggerated and the bizarre. Outside all schools as he is, it is puzzling to decide what category to put him in; if not among the precursors of Baroque then perhaps among the pre-Expressionists. What little we know of him shows him established in Munich from the year 1453 where he became important enough to qualify as a member of the City Council from 1467. A man isolated in his own time but an artist who, as far as character and technique are concerned, can take his place beside Baldung, Grünewald, Manuel and Ratgeb.

12 – In Ulrich Apt (*Triptych of the Crucifixion*, Augsburg, 1517), the sensibility remains medieval, even if the treatment of the forms, the unfolding of the landscape and the perspective appear modern. As for Leonard Beck, his Vienna *St. George* combines in a most curious way the narrative tone of the ancient legends and the simultaneous representation of several episodes in the same story in a single composition, with the heroic fancy of the later romances of chivalry and the poetic sentiment of the landscape.

13 – In Holbein's wake appear several Swiss artists of great interest whose chief merits are solid objectivity and fine pictorial qualities. The most famous and most remarkable of them should be mentioned first — Tobias Stimmer of Schaffhausen, a painter of stained glass windows and vast mural decorations at the Ritterhaus in his native town and in the palace of the Margrave Philip II in Baden-Baden. He worked a great deal in Italy where he made copies of Titian and Raphael and died at the comparatively early age of forty five in Strasburg in 1584, where he had decorated facades and supplied engravings to printers. A robustness which can be at once majestic and rustic *(Portraits of Banneret Jacob Schwytzer and his Wife*, Basle, 1564), a verve in his drawing which Rubens admired, a truthfulness composed of physical cheerfulness and moral distinction — such are the qualities that cause us to esteem Stimmer's talent and are perhaps responsible in part for the admiration we give to Holbein.

Along with him, Hans Hug Kluber (1535-1578), who like so many Basle artists, perished in the plague, commends himself to us above all for his curious *Family Portrait* (1559) which transposes the form of composition hitherto reserved for pious "Holy Family" paintings into the everyday reality of the middle-class home. Psychological curiosity is not Kluber's forte; in this "intimacy" of Provost Faesch, for example, he draws as much attention to the items of the meal which compose an accurate Still Life, succulent, if in a somewhat frigid way, as he does to the faces which all have a uniform family likeness that does not help us to differentiate their personalities.

As for Hans Bock the Elder (c. 1500-1623), born in Alsace, naturalized in Basle, a pupil and successor of Kluber and copyist of the paintings of Holbein for the Town Council, he was imprudent enough to use oil paint for his great murals where fresco would be the normal medium; and today no trace of them remains. It is therefore through his portraits *(Portrait of Councillor Hornlocher and his Wife*, Basle, 1577) that we know the conscientious, rather cold and reticent artist, before whom his models jealously kept their secrets to themselves.

Much more interesting is the disciple — it would be unjust to say imitator — of Niklaus Manuel Deutsch who is referred to by the name of Master H.F. His three portraits of men, of which the Basle one is the best, are signed with these initials, which could be those of Hans Franck of Basle or Hans Funk of Berne — the identification with Hans Fries having apparently been finally ruled out.

One might think that Dürer's genius would have inclined the painters of Nuremberg, his successors, to interest themselves likewise in the "potential" portrait, but it is not among his compatriots, in this respect at least, that his real disciples are to be found. His direct pupil, Georg Pencz (c. 1500-1550) appears more as a conscientious imitator of the Italians, no less in his murals than in his portraits, though the latter have a sharpness of expression, a contained vehemence, a kind of suppressed and controlled violence which owes nothing to Dürer, nor to the masters of the Peninsula whom he imitates elsewhere — in his mythological scenes for example. The portraits of *The Painter Schwetzer and his Wife* (Berlin) could have been influenced by Bronzino, but we are struck rather by their specifically German character. The same thing applies to the works of the Bavarian, Christoph Schwartz (1545-1592) who was familiar with the Venetians and even imitated them in his religious paintings; but there the resemblance ends. Any hint of Tintoretto, whom he loved so much and probably copied, has disappeared in the Munich *Family Portrait*, and his affinities with Hans Hug Kluber's portraiture are more in evidence.

The undisputed fact that in portraiture, the German character and tradition predominate even when in other genres the painters eagerly "Italianize", explains why the portrait can be regarded as the German art *par excellence* in the sixteenth century. Even when a cosmopolitan like Jakob Seisenegger (1505-1567), a portraitist of the Imperial Court, practises the eclecticism of a style which, like the Empire itself, wanted to be *European*, or when, for example, Hans Muelich (1516-1573) softens and whittles away the power of the German portrait until it becomes the art of the miniature.

In Nuremberg again we meet in the Beham family two painters, the more well known and better of whom — Barthel, also worked in Italy. Barthel Beham (1502-1540) remains very burdened with reminiscences of Dürer and Italian memories in such religious paintings as *The Discovery of the Cross* (Munich, 1530) which bears traces of the lessons received from Muelich in whose studio he worked at this period. But if we compare his portraits, that of *Count Palatine Johann* (Munich, 1533), for example, with this insufficiently individualized work, we discover a more sober, deeper, truer Barthel Beham; with him, as with so many others, Italianism stops short at the portrait.

In Conrad Faber (c. 1529-1551) who worked in Frankfort, provincialism, very much of a local school variety moreover, is especially noticeable in his somewhat heavy matter-of-factness and authenticity. The *Portrait of Georg Weiss* (Munich, 1533) which was one of the first pictures bought by Boisserée, is quite medieval in aspect and spirit, but of a healthy and refeshing vigor. The same is true of *The Portrait of a Woman* by Jacob Elsner (Berlin), dry, hard, almost as if wrought in precious metal, and of a moving solemnity in the irresistible gush of life perceptible in the expression which is at once so sincere and so human.

14 – A contemporary of Elsheimer, Johann Lyss (c. 1590-1630) also left Germany very young and joined the school of the Low Countries before settling down in Italy; but Johann Lyss' sole legacy from the teachings of those two countries was merely a brilliant and intriguing manner of treating genre scenes; his love of colour and *matière*, his Caravaggesque Baroque style are comparable to those of that other German of the Elsheimer group, Johann König (c. 1586-c. 1632).

Eclectic also was Frederik Sustris (c. 1540-1599), whose work has a sensual grace, a strange amalgam of Titian, Rubens and Gossaert.

Johann Rottenhammer (1564-1625) constituted a veritable crossroads of foreign aesthetics where Palma Vecchio and Jan Brueghel seem to have occupied the foreground; a very gifted, subtle artist, adept at turning everything to account, but to whom we can allot only a modest place in the history of German painting.

Quite as varied and of striking personality, seen through reflections of the various national schools with which he came into contact, Bartholomeus Spranger (1546-1611) is the perfect Mannerist, seduced by the unreality and fantasy which were so welcome in the circle of Rudolph II, at whose court Spranger spent his last years and finally died. He had known the masters of the School of Fontainebleau during his stay in France about 1565. Nowhere more than in his works do we become aware of the extent to which the *Mannerist Internationale* of the sixteenth century was able to adapt different aspects and create a quality of succulent grace.

At the court of Prague where the fantastic Rudolph gathered artists, authentic scholars and charlatans alike, all of whom were of equal interest to this man, curious about everything, from genuine wonders to extravagant trifles, there were to be found — apart from Spranger, the Emperor's painter — strange and delightful spirits such as Joseph Heinz (1564-1609) who was also a painter of the Chamber, Hans von

Aachen (1552-1616), trained in Venice and Rome, and Matthäus Goudelach, Hans' pupil and husband of Heintz's widow.

Mathias Scheits (c. 1630-1700) painted the same subjects as the Baroque eclectics, yet he contributed a personal spirit and very fine coloring. In him we find a particular taste for "grotesque" effects; his *Musician* (Hamburg) suggests a Nordic Magnasco, in love, like the real Magnasco, with broken forms that express the mixture of the burlesque and tragic elements in life.

Otto Wagenfedlt (c. 1610 — c. 1671), like Scheits a native of Hamburg, is one of the number of rare artists who found precisely in the tormented forms of Baroque and its dramatic chiaroscuro the immediate equivalent of the anguish which tortured their consciences. Two admirable paintings in the Kunsthalle at Hamburg which had been attributed to Scheits have now been hung under his name: *Death* (c. 1649-1651), a strange, tumultuous scene which unfolds round the bed of a dying man, and *The Original Sin* (1649-1651), which reveals an unusual iconographic *motif* : the Tree of Knowledge, represented by a skeleton — the symbol of Death — which forms the trunk.

Mathias Scheits had a worthy disciple in the person of his son, Andreas, who has a *Portrait of a Rabbi* and a *Still Life of Game* in Hamburg, both of which demonstrate the fidelity with which he followed his father's lessons and example.

15 – Ruthardt had belonged to the Guild of Painters during his stay in Antwerp (1663-1664). This monk delighted in hunting scenes and fights between animals, and it was only late in life that he was converted to a less profane art, and while in the Italian monastery of Abruzzi to which he had retired, substituted hermits and saints at prayer for wild beasts.

Wildmann, who ended his days in a monastery in Silesia, his native country, divided his admiration between Ruysdael and Rembrandt, whose landscapes he imitates, and Van Dyck, from whom his sacred pictures drew their inspiration. He had a fresh and exquisite feeling for nature, and the landscape painters of the eighteenth century who are dealt with later, mostly stem from him, although Rosa de Tivoli (his real name was Philipp Peter Roos, 1682-1705) also had a great influence on them as a "painter of ruins" and an animal painter.

This inclination to follow, albeit somewhat lazily, the examples of the Low Countries, appears to be general in the second half of the seventeenth century. It is noticeable again in the case of two other Silesians, Barthel Strobl (1591-1644) and Daniel Schultz (1615-1683). The latter knew his French contemporary masters in Paris where he spent some time, but the essential part of his life as an artist was passed in Russia and Poland. Southern Germany, on the other hand, gave birth to Johann Heinrich Schoenfeld, who established himself in Augsburg amongst the glorious Swabian traditions of the sixteenth century. He resembles the great Baroque decorators in his predilection for the animated architecture and landscapes which the Italians called "heroic pastorals".

There is not much to say about the painting of Joachim Sandrart (1608-1688), whose reputation as a historian of German painting surpasses his renown as an artist.

16 – Johann Martin Schmidt (1718-1801), who has been nicknamed "Kremserschmidt" on account of the fame he owed to his decorations in the parish church of Krems (1787); Franz Anton Sebastini (1725 ?-1789), called Schebesta by the Czechs for whom he worked a great deal; and Joseph Matthias Lassler (1698-1777), who was a pupil of Maulbertsch, also continued the spirit of Baroque up to the very threshold of the nineteenth century.

17 – When we see scholars replacing angels and saints in the compositions of Franz Sigrist (Lyzeum of Eger) and the cold allegories of Martin Knoller (1725-1804) substituting academism for passion, we regret that the prince's instructions were so literally followed and that the lessons of Winckelmann and Anton Rafael Mengs should have combined to dry up the powerful stream of Baroque.

There are certainly many good things in the works of Johann Christoph Frisch (1739-1845) — the grottoes in the Winter Garden of the castle of Paretz, for example — and Januarius Zick (1732-?), the son of Johann, displays a most agreable fantasy at Wiblingen and Rot, but the visionary current, so fascinating in his father, has dried up. Januarius is a typical "minor master" with all that term connotes, the virtuoso of the conversation-piece, Chodowiecki's rival in depictions of society life in the rationalist era and the *Aufklärung* — the age of Enlightenment.

18 – The fact that they enjoyed only local fame should not make us indifferent to straightforward and vigorous portrait-painters like J.G. Dathan (1703-1748) or Moritz Kellerhoven or again J.D. Preissler (1666-1737) who, with his three sons, practised engraving with great success. A Dane, J.G. Ziesenis (1716-1777), transplanted to Hanover; a Czech turned Franconian by adoption, Jan Kupetsky; a Pole, Daniel Chodowiecki (1726-1801); and a Hungarian trained in Paris, Crakow and Berlin, A. Manyoki (1673-1757), convey some idea of the cosmopolitanism of the German portrait school of the eighteenth century and of the ease with which they were assimilated into this foreign country so eager to absorb then. Ziesenis is the court painter *par excellence*, infatuated with rare elegance and a somewhat affected distinction. The Low Countries vied for him with Germany and kept him for a long time, so much did the sovereigns and nobility aspire to have their portraits painted by his hand. Ziesenis is guilty of an almost exaggerated artifice and grace, but his charm as a painter is genuine and represents the formalist aspect of Rococo. It is in this field too that we see the talent of Kupetzky who had the courage to leave Vienna despite his success there, because he considered that the Reformed Religion to which he belonged was being oppressed and badly treated. He spent twenty-two years in Italy where he felt greater freedom, and finally settled down in Nuremberg. Something of the *bravura* of the Italian Baroque painters, above all of Fra Galgario, passed into this artist possessed of authority and verve and the most productive portraitist of his time, who was however somewhat theatrical and too preoccupied with posing in front of his easel for the numerous self portraits which he executed.

19 – It is this feeling for nature that his many disciples have admired and imitated in him: Heinrich Reinhold (1788-1825), Carl Rottmann (1797-1850), Eberhard Georg Friedrich Wächter (1762-1852), Friedrich Wässmann (1805-1886), Heinrich Maria von Hess (1798-1863), Ernst Fries (1801-1833) and perhaps the best of the "Romanizing" romantics, Franz Hormy (1798-1824), whose career was suddenly interrupted at the age of twenty-six.

20 – The dazzling superiority of the masters of the "tragic landscape" should not make us unjust towards the merits of the "minor Romantics" whose predilection is for idyllic landscapes, as in the delightful Viennese painter, Ferdinand Georg Waldmüller (1793-1865), who so well expresses the simultaneously aristocratic and middle-class charm, simple yet refined, of "philistine" Austria. Waldmüller portrayed the promenades in the Viennese woods and bright mornings on the Prater with much grace and talent. A painter of portraits and intimate scenes, he personified the specifically Viennese aspect of Romanticism, just as the novelist-painter Adalbert Stifter with a temperament that abounded in discretion and emotion, evoked the topography of Salzburg and surroundings of Vienna while avoiding the merely *literary*. The Swiss landscape painters, among whom we also encounter another novelist-painter, Töpfer (1766-1847), manifest a new form of sensibility, both realist and poetic, of which Alexandre Calame (1810-1864), Maximilien de Meuron (1785-1868), François Diday (1802-1877) and a wealth of "minor" painters reflect its different aspects — tragic, familiar, naturalistic, idyllic.

21 – In its no less Düreresque detailed accuracy of treatment the *Portrait of Wilhelm von Schadow* by Carl Philipp Fohr (Kurpfälzisches Museum, Heidelberg, 1818) is, without any intentional archaism, imitation or pastische, a work much closer to the drawing of the sixteenth century than to the immediate precursors of Romanticism — Graff, Denner, Tischbein. The detachment of the Rococo or Neo-classical portrait disappears, and we see the return of the troubled gaze scrutinizing the inner and outer world, the *Faustian gaze* — which we shall come across again in the Expressionist portrait — and whose intensity completely holds the onlooker.

22 – Other painters — Arthur von Ramberg (1819-1875), Friedrich Kaulbach (1822-1903) — exaggerate the theatricality which existed in embryo in Piloty's "verism". No less theatrical are the genre-paintings of Wilhelm von Diez (1839-1907), who studied the Dutch a great deal and trans-

posed their technique in his scenes of popular life in Bavaria. Albert Anker of Berne (1831-1910) and the Tyrolean, Franz von Defregger (1835-1931) combine a popular spirit with confident and refined craftsmanship. The love of reality, in the form of a "slice of life", reappears after Defregger, but with an insistence on constructive and dynamic stylization, in the sober and vigorous interpreter of the Tyrolean people, Albin Egger-Lienz (1868-1926). Historical realism, threatened by theatrical distortion, foundered in paradoxical excess in the work of the Austrian, Hans Makart (1840-1884), with whom Vienna became infatuated, and whose vast, cumbersome decorations, dazzling in their sensuality, are in the style of old fashioned opera settings. Makart owed a great debt to Rubens; his taste coincided with that of the Vienna of the bankers, and his descendants, who are unworthy of him, were to plaster palace walls and casino ceilings with those artificial excesses of ribaldry, tinselled luxury and pastoral boudoir art for which he had set the example.

23 – We can estimate the value as a revelation of the Courbets and Millets exhibited in Munich, partly from the evolution in Leibl's work and partly in the landscape painters like Louis Eysen (1843-1899), Johann Sperl (1840-1914) and Rudolf Hirth du Frêne (1846-1916).

24 – Walter Gropius, *Idee und Aufbau des Staatlichen Bauhauses*, introduction to the volume entitled: *Das Staatlische Bauhaus in Weimar*, 1919-1923, Bauhaus-Verlag, Weimar-Munich.

25 – Quoted by Werner Haftmann.

LIST OF ILLUSTRATIONS

INDEX

CONTENTS